His uncles or His daddies? (sauna tale)

By:Anthony Hawkins

ISBN:978-1-304-04471-6

Cover Art By Anthony Hawkins

Dedicated to the gay and lesbian community.

Prologue

Tracey Johnson was a wild chick,the type that liked to rip and run the streets,and have multiple men in and out of her home,but her life would soon change,she would soon be a mother,tho she didn't know that herself just yet.

Tracey never took birth control,and rarely used condoms with her many male sex partners,she was the careless type,the dumb type,the type that thought hiv and aids was just a gay disease.Tracey woke up this morning,not having a clue that another life was growing inside of her,this was her first pregnancy ever in her young life.

Tracey opened her eyes slowly,as the sunlight met her eyelids,burning her pupils.Tracey quickly rushed over to her big window,and then slowly closed the curtains,blocking the sun from entering her now dim room.Tracey stood at her window for a few seconds,and then quickly rushed to the bathroom,feeling herself about to hurl.She placed her head over the toilet seat,holding her hair back in the process,and then flushing the toilet afterwards.Tracey knew something was wrong,but she had no clue what it was.

Tracey placed the toilet lid down,and then sat on it,thinking to herself long and hard,and then eventually going back to her everyday schedule,which was fuck a dude,and then rinse out her vagina,hoping that would stop her from getting pregnant,tho she would find out she was very wrong indeed.Tracey picked up her cell phone,wanting to call up one of her many men,wanting a little company for the rest of the evening.

Tracey didn't work,few of the men she slept with paid her for sex,that's how she made a living.What's up,you trying come over here daddy? Tracey spoke,after one of her guys answered their phone.Naw,im a little busy right now,but i be there a little later,the man spoke.Alright,i see you when you get here then,Tracey chuckled,ending the call afterwards.

Tracey left out the house around 12:00,and then came back around 1:45,leaving out to run a few errands.

Girl you had me waiting out this motherfucker for a minute,why you tell a nigga to come over,and then leave the fucking house? A tall dark and deep voice man spoke,his eyes on Tracey.You told me you was coming over a little later,so i left the fuck out,i aint know you was coming this early,you aint my damn daddy,i aint gotta explain nothing to your black ass,Tracey spoke.Stop talking to me crazy girl,i aint dem other niggas you be fucking with,alright,im going tell you that shit straight up,the man spoke,his voice stern.Whatever Mike,i aint call your ass over here for no bullshit,i just need some company nigga,Tracey smirked,placing her keys into the front door of her apartment,gently easing herself in,as Mike eased in behind her,closing the door behind him.

Tracey dropped her keys on her dining room table,and then grabbed Mike by his waist as she turned toward him.Naw,chill with that,i told you i dont do that dirty shit,we can fuck once you stop fucking all dem other niggas,i dont wanna be jumping in and out of pussy three or four more niggas then been in,give that shit to the birds,i just came here to chill with you,Mike spoke,a frown on his face.

Im starting to think your ass kind of fruity,You have been to jail,Tracey snickered.Go ahead with that bullshit,dont ever fucking disrespect me like that again man,i dont play that gay shit,Mike frowned,an angry expression on his mug.Tell the truth Mike,you ever fucked a nigga in prison,im just saying,aint no females in there? Tracey chuckled.The shit you saying is dangerous,motherfuckers get shot for saying shit like that,but on the real,i let a nigga suck my dick once,not when i was in the joint tho,i was just trying get a nut tho,that's fucking it,a mouth is a mouth,you better keep this shit between us too man,Mike spoke,giving Tracey the stare.

Tracey chuckled in response,her arms tightly around Mike's waist.

Mike didn't take advantage of Tracey's promiscuous nature the way many other men did,tho Tracey was eager to get him into bed with her.Mike was more of a friend rather than a lover to Tracey,tho they both had mutual attraction for each other.Mike stood six feet and two inches tall,had smooth dark brown skin,and lips that seemed as if they were made for kissing,his face handsome and neatly shaven,tho he seemed like the rough type,the kind of guy that would pull out a gun and shoot you,just because you gave him the wrong look.

Mike was a thug,but had a gentle side to him.Mike's rough nature was a product of his rough upbringing.You can give the dick to dem other bitches,but not me huh? Tracey smirked.I know you fucked that bitch Tamika down the street,she then told everybody on the block,she think you her nigga or something,Tracey spoke,her arms still around Mike's waist.Tamika dont have niggas running in and outta her house like your ass do,that's why i fucks with her,but that broad run her damn mouth too much,i only fucked her one time,now she think im supposed to marry her motherfucking ass or some shit,bitches be tripping,Mike murmured.

Was her pussy good? Tracey questioned Mike with a smile.Hell yea! Mike smiled.Shit probably aint better then mine,i tell you that,Tracey boasted.Probably aint,but that shit aint as loose as yours either,Mike chuckled.

Tracey chuckled along and then unwrapped her arms from around Mike's waist,heading over to her sofa,her right hand over her stomach.You alright,what the fuck wrong with you? Mike questioned Tracey.Tracey could feel a quick and sudden thump against her stomach,she flinched.I hope aint none of dem niggas give me something,Tracey spoke silently as Mike headed towards her.You need to stop all that whoring around,that shit aint cool,this should be your motherfucking lesson,Mike spoke to Tracey,sitting next to her.You got pains somewhere or something? Mike questioned Tracey with concern.

Naw,not pains,i just feel funny,Tracey explained.You feel funny right here,or right here? Mike questioned as he placed his left hand on different places and angles of Tracey's body,trying to search for the spot where Tracey felt funny.Naw,it's in this area,Tracey spoke,placing her hand over her stomach again.Lift your shirt up,Mike ordered Tracey.

Tracey pulled her shirt up,revealing a slight bulge in her stomach.Mike exhaled as he examined the bulge.Shawty one of dem niggas then knocked you up,no bullshit,you need to get that shit checked out asap,Mike explained,shaking his head in the process.I hope fucking not,i surely fucking hope not,Tracey murmured in disappointment.You dont use condoms with dem niggas? Mike questioned Tracey,his face confused.Sometimes,but when i dont i make dem niggas pull out,Tracey explained.

You trifling ass hell man,shit,im glad i aint hit the skins yet,Mike chuckled softly.

Fuck you,you feel like running me to the corner store right quick,i gotta get a test,for real,i better not be fucking pregnant,Tracey muttered,having fear of becoming a mother.Tracey and Mike headed to the local corner store that was just a few blocks down the street from where Tracey lived,and once they got back,Tracey found out her life changing news,that she was going to be a mother soon.

Chapter 1

I cant believe this shit,one of dem niggas paying child support,Tracey mumbled,her head resting inside her palms.Get a motherfucking abortion,i give you the money,it's this chick that do the shit not too far from here,Mike spoke,trying to comfort Tracey.

Two tears departed from Tracey's eyes as she checked the positive pregnancy test again.I think im too far gone for a abortion,how the fuck am i going support this baby? Fuck! Tracey spoke,throwing the pregnancy test against her wall.You put yourself in this shit,letting dem niggas fuck without a rubber,and now you got a little boy or little girl on the way,and i aint trying be nobody daddy,so dont think im going be helping you wit that little motherfucker,Mike spoke,his eyes on Tracey.

Fool chill the fuck out,i aint ask you nothing,i think i know who the father is,it gotta be either Jarrelle's or P's,Tracey spoke,her face blank.Deep down Tracey didn't know who was the father of her unborn child.

The months passed and passed,and Tracey had eventually given birth to her child,a baby boy she named Jayden,Jayden Johnson.Tracey had found out who her babys father was over time,it was Jarrelle,Jarrelle was Jayden's biological father,tho in the beginning he resisted to take a dna test.Jarrelle was barely a part of Jayden's life,and hardly wanted anything to do with Tracey,but Tracey still managed without him.

Baby Jayden was adorable,having one of the cutest faces you could ever see,with soft brown skin that felt like silk,and innocent looking eyes,eyes that made you melt.Tracey rocked baby Jayden back and forth in her arms as she sat on the sofa,her eyes on the television.Tracey placed baby Jayden in his crib after hearing a thump at her front door.Who is it? Tracey spoke as she closed the robe she wore over her night clothes.It's Mike,open the damn door,it's freezing out this bitch,Mike spoke.Tracey opened the door,and then allowed Mike to come in,closing and locking her door as Mike entered.

Mike was somewhat attracted to Tracey,but she wasn't exactly his type,and now he had even more of a reason to visit her,he adored her son.

Mike didn't really care for children,but Jayden changed his whole aspect.It's nice and toasty in this joint,where your little man at? Mike spoke,taking off his coat,and then tossing it on the sofa.He in the room,he probably sleep now,Tracey spoke,heading towards her room to check on baby Jayden.Mike followed behind Tracey,and then eased himself pass her to get to Jayden's crib.Mike reached out toward baby Jayden,wanting to pick the baby boy up.Hell no,dont touch my baby wit cha cold ass hands! Tracey spoke,a slight frown on her face.Mike paused,and then pulled his arms back,a frown on his face.

Whatever,i just wanted to hold little man,you trippin,Mike spoke,and then sitting himself on the edge of Tracey's bed.I didn't say you couldn't hold him,just wait until your hands warm up,and wash dem motherfuckers too,I know the nasty bitches you be messin wit,Tracey smirked at Mike.Mike sighed,and headed into the bathroom,washing his hands,and then heading back towards Jayden's crib.

Come here little man,Mike whispered as he gently scooped Jayden into his arms.Mike rocked Jayden back and forth in his arms,and then began walking around with him.Tracey could see that Mike was good with kids,tho he didn't have any of his own.Tracey used Mike to her advantage,taking the little time she had to herself to take a quick nap.Two hours had passed.Tracey headed into the living area,spotting Mike on the sofa with Jayden sleeping in his arms.Alright,give me my damn baby,Tracey uttered,reaching towards Jayden as he rested in Mike's big arms.

Tracey got her hands halfway around baby Jayden's small body,but then stopped,hearing a loud thump at her door.The thumps awoken Jayden,causing him to cry out.Damn,he was sleep too,Tracey sighed,her face disappointed.Tracey headed towards the front door,and then pushed her eye towards the peephole.P why you knocking so damn loud,you know my baby be sleepin,Tracey spoke,apparently knowing who the knocker was.Tracey opened her door as the man P entered,dropping his coat on the floor as he entered.

Damn nigga,have some respect dawg,you dropping your shit on the floor,and you woke little man up,Mike explained,trying to get Jayden to go back to sleep.How was i supposed to know that little nigga was sleep? I just came over here to bang his moms,P smiled.You know you smashing it too nigga,P chuckled.Dont be saying shit like that in front of my son P,Tracey spoke out.The little dude dont know what im saying,so chill,P smirked.Can you watch Jayden for me a little longer

Mike? I be back,Tracey whispered as P headed into her room.

Do what chu do,that's nasty as fuck tho,bringing all these different niggas around your son like that,you a mother now man,that shit aint cool,Mike frowned.

Stay out my business,im a grown ass woman Mike,i hear the same shit from Ms Glenda old ass,yea,im a mother,but i gotta have a life too,Tracey spoke.Aint nothing wrong with having a life,but dont bring that shit around your son,that's all im saying,shit like that can mentally scar the little dude,Mike explained,finally getting Jayden back to sleep.Ya'll going stop insulting my mothering skills,that's my motherfucking baby,Tracey spoke,knowing Mike's words were getting to her.Get cha ass in here girl! P yelled out.

Tracey rolled her eyes at Mike,and then headed into the other room with P,shutting the door behind her.Mike turned up the tv,trying to tune out the moans that escaped Tracey's bedroom,still rocking baby Jayden in his arms.

The hours passed.P and Tracey finally exited the bedroom,P zipping up his pants as he exited.You said you was going give me a couple of dollas,i gave you some nookie,so where my shit? Tracey smiled at P.I got a baby mama to take care of,im out shawty,P murmured,unphased by Tracey's words.Fuck nigga,i need the money,you gave me your motherfucking word! Tracey shouted at P.You trippin man,P spoke,and then turning his back to Tracey,ignoring her.Come on P,i need the money,Tracey begged,gently placing her hand above P's shoulder,trying to persuade him.

Get the fuck off me girl! P shouted,backhanding Tracey,causing her to fall violently into the bedroom door.Dawg,little man sleep,ya'll need to cut that shit out cuz,you need to roll out man,on the real! Mike yelled at P,forgetting that he had raised his own voice also.Man shut the fuck up,and tell your sister and whoever to suck my dick! P yelled at Mike.

Look,look,calm down P,let's talk baby,Tracey begged again.P and Tracey entered the bedroom again,shutting the door behind them.Just give me something,please P,Tracey begged again,hoping P would take pity on her.At least do it for Jayden,he need milk,Tracey pleaded again.Man fuck you and your son bitch! P yelled at Tracey,having no remorse for her.As a matter of fact,give me some head,and i might give you something,P spoke,his eyes buried in Tracey's cleavage.Naw,im not falling for that shit again nigga,Tracey spoke.Fuck that,im horny again,you going give that pussy up! P shouted,tossing Tracey on the bed,and then forcing himself on top of her as she screamed.

P began to smack Tracey continuously across the face,and then began to punch her,eventually causing her nose and mouth to bleed.Mike heard the commotion,and then quickly but gently sat baby Jayden on the sofa as he ran towards Tracey's bedroom door,kicking it in.Get the fuck out nigga! It's a fucking child out there man! Mike shouted,grabbing and then throwing P from Tracey.Tracey curled herself into the corner of her bed as Mike dragged P out by his neck.

Get the fuck out dawg! Mike spoke,shoving P towards the front door.

Dawg you about to get dealt wit! P yelled at Mike.Mike grabbed his coat,and then pulled a fully loaded black steel gun from the inside pockets of it,cocking it,and then aiming it at P.Like i said nigga,get the fuck out! Mike shouted,his nostrils flaring,and his gun pointing at P.I got chu nigga,you going be six feet under,im out for now dawg,P murmured,grabbing up his coat,and then leaving out the front door.

Mike slammed the front door behind P as P exited the apartment building.Mike put the locks on the door and then tucked his gun back into his coat pocket,then quickly rushed over to Jayden,cradling

Jayden in his arms as he headed back into Tracey's room.Mike gave Tracey a blank expression and then gently placed Jayden into his crib.That little dude right there,he need a mother,be one,Mike said,pointing his finger to Jayden,his face angered,he was clearly pissed off.

Here,dont use it on dumb shit,make sure most of that is used on Jayden,Mike spoke,dropping a couple of hundred dollar bills on Tracey's bed,and then leaving out her bedroom.Tracey quickly checked in on Jayden,and then headed into the bathroom,seeing her bruised face in the bathroom mirror.Tracey dabbed her face with a hot rag,and then began to cry on the bathroom floor,tears streaming down her face.Tracey began ravaging the bathroom,angry at P,angry at what he had done to her.Tracey finally snapped back to her senses,and then cleaned herself up,shrugging into clean clothes,and then throwing her previous clothes in the trashcan,because they reminded her of P.

Tracey headed back into her bedroom,seeing no signs of baby Jayden,she flipped.

Tracey ran into the living area,where she saw Jayden being fed a warm bottle by Mike,that calmed her nerves.Little man ok,i got him,Mike explained,and then giving Jayden a kiss on the forehead.Tracey saw the difference between Mike and P,and she saw it clearly.

Three days had passed,and Tracey was now searching for a job,realizing she had to change her lifestyle very quickly.Mike helped Tracey out with baby Jayden,giving her money for the basics,and even babysitting Jayden on occasions,doing things that Jayden's actual father should have.

Sh,hush that noise,you alright,you here wit big Mike,i aint going hurt chu little dude,your moms be back,Mike whispered to Jayden,cradling him in his arms.Jayden took to Mike very well,just as much as Mike took to him,giggling and smiling everytime Mike was around.Im going teach ya little ass how to fight,Mike spoke,placing Jayden on the floor.Come on,stand up,Mike spoke to Jayden,standing Jayden to his little feet.Jayden could walk just a little now,but still stumbled every now and then.

Mike placed the sofa pillows all around Jayden as a precaution,incase Jayden fell.Mike cuffed his big hands into fists,and playfully swung them back and forth,but away from Jayden,Jayden began to giggle in response,and then began to clap his small hands together in a tender baby laughter.

Mike chuckled and then kissed Jayden on the cheek,scooping Jayden into his arms again.Mike had a somewhat fatherly love for Jayden.

It was now time for Jayden's bath,and Mike decided to join him,not wanting Jayden to bath alone,and wanting to bath himself as well.Mike felt that he could kill two birds with one stone.Mike turned on the shower head,and then checked the water temperature,and then peeled Jayden out of his baby sleeper,and then taking off all of his clothes as well,allowing the water to rain down on both he and Jayden's nude bodies,but keeping the water away from Jayden's face.

There was a loud banging sound against the front door,it caught Mike's ears.Mike cradled Jayden into his arms and then strutted towards the door,a bold and manly strut,he didn't bother to place clothes on he or Jayden's wet naked bodies,he was just that bold.Who is it?! You banging like the motherfucking police! Mike spoke,flinging the door open,revealing himself and Jayden to the knocker.Who you? Mike spoke to the male visitor,his face annoyed,but confused.Im Jarrelle,where the fuck is Tracey? The man spoke.She out dawg,i heard her talk about you before tho,you little man pops right? Mike spoke,his eyes on Jarrelle's face.

Yea,i am.Cuz im going keep it real,why the fuck is you and my little dude naked man?! Jarrelle spoke,his voice stern.Nigga dont even trip,i needed to shower,and little man needed a bath too,so shit,i took a shower wit him,i aint trying ass jack your son,so get that shit out cha head dawg,Mike explained.Look,get my son shit packed and give him to me,i cant have my son around the bullshit Tracey bringing in this motherfucker,yea,i heard about ya'll arguing and fighting and shit,neighbors talk dawg,ya'll can kill each other if ya'll want,but not around my motherfucking son cuz,Jarrelle spoke,his face angered.

Nigga shut your ass up,this nigga name P gave your baby moms a ass whooping,not me motherfucker,let's get that straight,Mike frowned,his pecks flexing just a little.So now you wanna be a father? Nigga get the fuck outta here,Mike spoke.I been the only man in this little dudes life so far,where you been at dawg? Mike murmured.Dawg listen,give me my motherfucking son,this the last time im going say the shit,Jarrelle spoke,his voice raising.

Come on little homey,we going catch a cold in this bitch,Mike whispered softly into baby Jayden's ear,and then kissing him softly on the forehead,deliberately ignoring Jarrelle's words.Nigga if you didn't have my son in your arms i would seriously two piece your ass,no lie,Jarrelle muttered.And then you kissing on my little dude dawg,that's that faggot shit,you aint his motherfucking father,Jarrelle uttered,anger in his voice.We going go get your bottle ready little J,Mike spoke,calling Jayden by his nickname,and then kissing him again,knowing he was pissing Jarrelle off.

Mike turned his back to Jarrelle,exposing his tight naked ass cheeks to Jarrelle,and then kicked the door shut,placing the locks on the door again.Jarrelle banged and banged against the front door as Mike got himself and Jayden fully clothed again.Mike sat himself and baby Jayden on the sofa,and then turned on the tv,muting Jarrelle's voice with the voices of cartoons as Jayden relaxed quietly in his arms,too entertained by the cartoons to notice his fathers voice outside the front door.

The hours passed,and Jarrelle had finally given up,no longer knocking on the front door or shouting.Keys entered into the front door,it was Tracey,she was finally home.Mike! What the hell happened?! Tracey yelled,searching the house for Mike and Jayden.What chu talkin about? Mike yarned,sitting himself up in the bed as Jayden slumbered in his crib.Jarrelle called me! Tracey shouted.And? Mike said stiffly.Why you causing trouble wit him,when you know i need all the help i can get?! Tracey spoke,her arms folded.Man fuck that nigga,it's funny how he trying be a father now,i been there for that boy since he was born,and he just trying pack the little homey up and leave wit him? Mike spoke,standing to his feet.

I understand where you coming from Mike,but you not Jayden's father,ok,Tracey muttered,her face guilty.Tracey's words were like knives piercing through Mike's skin.You taking it there Tracey,alright,that's some hurtful ass shit man,im not trying stop J from seeing his father,but nigga could've ran off wit the little dude,and your ass would never see ya damn son again,i seen the shit happen,im from the streets man,Mike spoke,his eyes glassy.

I need you to give Jayden some time to know his real father Mike,Jayden need his father to teach him the streets,it's rough out there,you know that,im changing the locks tomorrow,i need you gone for a couple of months or longer,i dont wanna argue,just leave Mike,Tracey said softly.Cool,im out,but yous a sorry ass motherfucker man,fuck you Tracey,Mike spoke,heading towards baby Jayden's crib,giving baby Jayden a silent kiss on the forehead before heading towards the front door.

Fuck you Tracey,fuck you man,I fucking love that little boy,and you pull some shit like this,Mike spoke as he pulled the front door open,two tears slowly sliding down his face.Mike gave baby Jayden one more glance,and then exited the apartment,letting the door slam behind him.Tracey felt guilty,but wanted Jayden's father in his life,but most of all,in hers.Tracey hovered over Jayden's crib,where she spotted a small tear drop on Jayden's cheek,it belonged to Mike.

Three months had passed,and Jarrelle had moved in with Tracey and

Jayden,but left three months later,leaving Tracey and Jayden high and dry again,even stealing money from Tracey's purse.Tracey fell back in rent payments,and not having a job just yet made things worse,Tracey called Mike for help eventually,tho Mike was still deeply hurt and angry,he still came to the rescue,if it meant helping baby Jayden.Mike spent a year with Jayden and Tracey,but once again,Tracey kicked Mike out of Jayden's life once she found a new man,a man that didn't really care about her or Jayden,even sniffing cocaine with his homeboys

while baby Jayden sat in his lap,and
the cycle continued.

Chapter 2

Eighteen years had passed,and many
things had changed.Tracey had
allowed P to move in with her and
Jayden,even after the distress he
caused her,and P regulated just
about everything in the house,tho he
didn't pay any bills,nor contributed
anything to the apartment.

Jayden was now an adult,18 years old,he was no longer baby Jayden,but still had his innocent eyes,eyes that made you melt.Jayden had a good head on his shoulders,tho the environment he was in wasn't always pleasant and to his liking.Jayden had grown to be a very handsome young man,having smooth abs and pecks,toned legs,a round firm ass,firm muscles,and teeth that were as white as snow.Girls adored Jayden,but he didn't return the favor,Jayden liked women,but just not in the same way they liked him,he was more interested in dating people of his own gender,and they were interested in dating him too,tho Tracey nor P knew this.

Jayden where your moms at nigga?! P shouted as he headed towards Jayden's bedroom door.She left out,she said she be back,Jayden spoke,his voice now mature.Open the door,i cant fucking hear you! P spoke.She left out,she said she be back,Jayden said again as he opened his bedroom door slightly,meeting P's stare.Alright,P said calmly.That dude been in ya room for a minute now,dont that nigga gotta place of his own,why the fuck he always over here? P spoke,his eyes peeping through the crack of Jayden's bedroom door.

He about to leave in a minute,it's cool,Jayden spoke,his face nervous.Naw,tell that nigga he gotta leave now,as a matter of fact,i'll tell the nigga! P spoke as he pushed his way through Jayden's bedroom door,causing Jayden to stumble slightly to the side.Yo,what the fuck was ya'll little niggas in here doing? P questioned Jayden in a stern voice,his nose spread,seeing Jayden's male friend quickly pull up his underwear.We was just chillin man,my boy about to roll out,Jayden quickly spoke out,butterflies in his stomach.Little nigga you lying like a motherfucker,P spoke,giving Jayden the evil eye.

You think im stupid dawg,you was sucking this nigga dick,wasn't you? P yelled at Jayden.Little faggot ass motherfuckers,i should beat the shit outta both of ya'll! P spoke,his fingers now balled up into fists.Delonte just go man,i get at chu a little later,Jayden spoke,wanting his friend to leave the house before anything transpired.Delonte headed towards the door,but was stopped by

P.Delonte tried to head for the door again,but was punched by P,falling to the hardwood floor afterwards.You aint going nowhere you faggot ass nigga! P shouted out,now kicking Delonte in his stomach and side.

Chill P! Jayden spoke,grabbing P by his arms,trying to restrain P,seeing that P was putting serious damage to Delonte.P shoved Jayden off of him,and then finally let up on Delonte.Delonte quickly jumped to his feet,and ran out of Jayden's bedroom,his right hand holding his stomach.Get cha ass outta here motherfucker! P yelled,following behind Delonte.Delonte quickly exited the front door,and then darted out of the apartment building,fearing for his safety.P slammed the front door and then placed the locks on the door.Jayden backed into his room,fear on his face.

I aint checking for you little nigga,but just wait until your moms get home motherfucker,P spoke,and then slowly headed into the other direction.Jayden sat on his bed,and then began to ponder,his hands shaking,he had the jitters.Jayden could hear keys twisting in the locks of the front door.Tracey was entering the apartment,two bags hanging from her left arm.What's going on,why you so quiet? Tracey questioned Jayden as she headed towards his bedroom door,knowing something was bothering him.Im cool ma,Jayden spoke silently,his nerves getting the best of him.Im going tell you why that motherfucker quiet,him and that other nigga was doing some gay shit up in here,that's why he quiet! P shouted,and then walking into full view of Tracey and Jayden.

What he talkin about Jayden? Tracey questioned,her face confused.Delonte was over today,P thought me and him was doing something,some sex type shit,Jayden murmured silently,guilt in his face.Boy you know i dont play that gay shit in this house,you know what the bible say about that type of shit,Tracey spoke,her voice stern.Im not mad tho,trust me,i know you know betta than that J,and Delonte dont seem like he swing that way either,Tracey spoke,and then caressed Jayden's cheek,putting a smile on Jayden's face.P wanted to confront Jayden in front of Tracey,wanting to make an example out of him.

Naw,hold up,this shit aint over,if you aint going put this little nigga in line i will! P yelled at Tracey.P,he said nothing happened between him and Delonte,stop making something out of nothing,Tracey explained softly.Man,fuck this! P yelled,yanking his belt off his pants,pushing Tracey out of the way as he headed towards Jayden,and then slamming Jayden's bedroom door in her face,locking himself and Jayden inside.

P began to beat Jayden with the belt as Jayden screamed out.P what the fuck is wrong wit chu?! Open the motherfucking door,dont touch my fucking baby P! Tracey screamed,banging her fist against the bedroom door.Tracey could now hear Jayden whimpering in pain,crying out each time the belt hit him.Shut cha faggot ass up! Tracey heard P yell at Jayden.Each lash P gave to Jayden sent chills through Tracey's body,tears began to stream down her face.

P finally exited Jayden's room,pulling his belt back around the waist of his pants as he headed to the other room.Tracey quickly entered Jayden's room,spotting Jayden curled up on the floor.Tho there were no bruises left on Jayden,he could still feel the sting of P's belt.Tracey quickly placed Jayden in her arms,as if he were still a baby,tho he was her baby,her baby boy.Tears began to fall from Jayden's eyes as Tracey caressed and soothed him,until they both fell asleep.

Jayden awoke the next morning with Tracey laying next to him,her eyes close shut.Jayden shook Tracey's shoulder,trying to get her to awaken.Tracey slowly opened her eyes,and then stretched herself out,giving Jayden a smile as she turned towards his gaze.Go get some more sleep ma,im cool now,Jayden whispered to Tracey.You sure you ok baby? Tracey questioned,her eyes weary.Yea,im cool,Jayden answered clearly,a soft smile on his face.Ok baby,i be back to check on you,Tracey spoke,slowly leaving out of Jayden's room and into her own.

Jayden's smile faded as he thought about the beating his mothers boyfriend P gave him.Jayden headed to the bathroom,and then checked himself in the mirror.He then turned on the faucet,and allowed the sink to fill with water,splashing the water on his face,and then drying his face with a cloth.Jayden then headed into the living area,spotting P on the sofa,pissy drunk,a liquor bottle next to the sofa he slept on.Jayden headed into his room,and then grabbed his coat from out of his closet,snatching up his keys also,and then silently eased out of the front door,hoping not to awaken P.

Jayden sat outside for hours,taking in the fresh air,and then headed back inside,hearing P and Tracey arguing,even before he entered the apartment.Get out P! Tracey yelled.I aint going no motherfucking where! P yelled back at Tracey.Jayden was used to hearing P and Tracey argue,tho he hated it deep down.Jayden silently entered his bedroom,shutting his door quietly behind him,and then grabbed his earphones from his dresser,turning his mp3 player to full blast,wanting to tune out all of the noise that came from P and Tracey.

Jayden rested himself on the floor,and then drifted asleep after awhile,his earphones falling from his ears.Jayden awoke a few hours later,now seeing the moonlight shining outside of his window,the sky pitch black.Jayden sat himself up,and then placed his earphones and mp3 player back on his dresser.Jayden still had on the same clothes from yesterday,and now he wanted to change into something else,not having the energy to do so right after he was beaten by P the night before.Jayden silently exited his bedroom,and then headed into the bathroom that was near his room,bringing a clean pair of jeans and a t shirt in the bathroom with him.Jayden soaped himself,and then let the water rinse him off afterwards,shrugging into his jeans and t shirt after he was done.

Jayden eased back into his bedroom,and then slipped his feet into a pair of nike shoes,and then placed his coat on,tucking his mp3 into the pockets.Jayden wanted to get away from the apartment,just for awhile.Jayden grabbed his keys,and then headed out the front door,placing on the bottom lock as he exited.

Jayden placed his earphones into his ears,and then headed down the street,once leaving the apartment building.Jayden didn't focus on anything but the music playing in his ears,and the street lights that dimly lit the night.Jayden accidently bumped into a tall man as he roamed the streets,too distracted by the music playing in his ears.Oh shit,my bad man! Jayden quickly apologized to the man,afraid of what the mans reaction might be.It's cool dawg,the tall and dark man smiled thinly at Jayden.Little dude you look familiar,you from around here dawg? The man questioned Jayden in his deep voice.Yea,all my life man,Jayden answered.Damn you look familiar,i seen you somewhere before dawg,i just dont know where? The man spoke again,his eyes carefully studying Jayden's face.

What's your name little dude? The man questioned Jayden.No disrespect,but i dont give out my name to just anybody,not trying be disrespectful tho man,Jayden murmured.I respect that dawg,but chu still look familiar tho,i see you around little homey,my name Mike,big Mike,the man spoke,giving Jayden one more glance before heading down the street,eventually fleeing Jayden's sight.

Jayden thought the man Mike was attractive,but scary as hell too.Jayden had no clue that Mike was the same man that fed,bathed,and babysat him when he was just a child.Mike had no clue who Jayden was either,not seeing Jayden in years,only seeing Jayden on and off,year after year,and then soon he didn't see Jayden at all,something Tracey was responsible for,Tracey and the many men she slept around with.Jayden headed back home after a couple of hours,and then quietly eased himself back into the house,turning his keys gently in the locks as he entered.

The apartment was pitch black,only the kitchen light was on.Jayden couldn't see anything with the lights off,so Jayden switched the lights on,and there was P,sitting on the sofa,his legs gapped open,and a bottle of liquor tilting from his hand.Where the fuck you been at motherfucker? P muttered,his eyes on Jayden.Jayden was shocked,not knowing that P was going to be waiting silently in the dark when he got back to the apartment.I just went out for a minute,i just wanted to chill to myself,Jayden stuttered,his speech altered by his fear of P.I just went out for a minute,i just wanted to chill to myself,P mocked Jayden,making his voice squeaky.

Nigga ask permission before you leave this motherfucking house,just because you grown now dont mean you can come and go as you motherfucking please,P spoke to Jayden,giving Jayden a mean mug in the process.My bad man,but i just went around the corner,Jayden explained to P.You went over that nigga house,didn't you? P questioned Jayden.What's his name,Delonte right? Faggot ass nigga,i hope he enjoyed that ass whooping i gave him,P spoke,taking another sip of his liquor,and then placing his eyes on Jayden again.Dawg im going tell you like this,if i catch that little nigga in here wit chu again,shit going get ugly dude,P spoke calmly,standing to his feet.

I got chu man,Where my ma at? Jayden questioned P.She went out for a minute,but dont worry about her,we talking nigga,man to man,P spoke,walking slowly towards Jayden.Remember what the fuck i told you nigga,let me catch that nigga in here again,watch what i do,P spoke as he and Jayden stood face to face,P standing slightly above Jayden.Alright man,you made your point dawg,i feel you,Jayden spoke to P.Nigga what? P said swiftly.I wasn't trying disrespect you P,i was just letting you know that i got chu,i feel where you coming from,Jayden spoke,his nerves rushing through his body.Fuck that nigga,you was trying be smart motherfucker,i aint stupid dawg! P yelled at Jayden,slinging his liquor bottle to the floor.

You going learn motherfucker,bring ya ass here little motherfucker,i told you to stop fucking disrespecting me! P shouted,yanking Jayden by his collar,and then dragging him into the bathroom,shutting the door behind them.P go ahead man! Jayden spoke out,knowing P was about to do something cruel to him.Get the fuck off me P! Jayden yelled,struggling to break away from P's strong grip.Save all that yelling nigga! P shouted at Jayden.You aint doing shit you pussy ass nigga,sit cha ass down bitch ass nigga! P shouted,smacking Jayden to the tile floor of the bathroom.

I had to take a piss,and now i found the perfect motherfucking toilet,P chuckled,pulling down his pants and underwear.P then chucked his penis into his hand,and then began to urinate on Jayden,soaking Jayden in his urine.Fuck you man,fuck you P! Jayden shouted.Jayden balled up his fists,every part of him wanting to attack P.You can ball up your fists all you want motherfucker,hit me,and watch me crack your motherfucking face little nigga,P said in a clear voice,shaking the last drop of urine from his penis onto Jayden.

P pulled up his pants and underwear again,and then headed out the bathroom like nothing ever happened,leaving Jayden soaked in his urine.Jayden sat on the bathroom floor,his hands shaking,and his anger boiling.Jayden's clothes stuck to his body,soaked in P's hot urine.

Jayden slowly eased himself up from the floor,and then began tearing his clothes from his body,throwing them into the bathroom trashcan,and then quickly turning on the shower head,stepping into the bathtub,where he washed away P's urine from his body.Jayden headed into his bedroom after he was done with his shower,placing on a thin shirt and a pair of sweat pants.Jayden tucked his face into his palms,and then sighed silently as he sat on his bed.Jayden could hear someone knocking at the front door of the apartment,even tho his bedroom door was closed.

Jayden was about to go answer the front door,but P beat him to the punch.Jayden was glad he didn't answer the front door,because it was two of P's homeboys,and they were just as vile as P.What's good motherfuckers? Jayden heard P speak to his friends.Jayden knew that P and his homeboys were going to start acting like fools once they settled in and got a couple of drinks in their system,so he took a nap,hoping P's friends would be gone by the time he woke up.

Jayden awoke from his nap two hours later,and unfornately P's friends were still there in the apartment,raising hell like he knew they would.Jayden could smell the scent of marijuana creeping in from under the cracks of his bedroom door,the scent came from P and his friends,they were smoking.Jayden didn't want to leave his room,but he was thirsty as hell.Jayden headed out to the kitchen and then poured himself a glass of water,ignoring P and his friends,hoping neither of the men harrassed him like they usually did.What's up little Jayden,i heard you like it up the ass?! One of P's friends snickered,P and the other friend snickering along.

Yea,whatever,Jayden mumbled,now done with his glass of water.I heard ya mama like it up the ass too,the man continued to harrass Jayden,as Jayden ignored him.Naw,im just playin wit cha soft ass,the man chuckled,his eyes on Jayden.Jayden turn your ass around and speak to the man! P demanded.Jayden turned himself around slowly,and then met the mans gaze.Hey Lenny,Jayden said to P's friend nonchalantly.Trey sittin right there,say hi to Trey,show some respect nigga,P ordered Jayden.What's good Trey? Jayden said hesitantly to P's other friend,becoming annoyed.

Where ya punk ass pops Jarrelle? Lenny chuckled.Who knows man? Jayden spoke calmly,wishing Lenny and the others would shut the fuck up.Shit,me,Trey,and P could've been your daddy nigga,ya moms was a fast ass,Lenny snickered,taking a puff of the marijuana that rested inbetween his fingers.Jayden turned towards the front door,hearing someone enter the house,it was Tracey.Hey Lenny,hey Trey,what chall doing here so late? Tracey spoke.Ya'll hoes probably at home waiting on ya'll,but yet chall here,stinking up my damn house wit that weed,Tracey murmured,standing beside Jayden,her arm around his shoulder.

Hey baby,Tracey whispered to Jayden,squeezing his arm gently.Hey ma,Jayden whispered back.P grabbed Tracey gently by her other arm,pulling her away from Jayden,and next to him and his homeboys.Give me some lovin girl,P whispered in Tracey's ear,groping her behind,and then kissing her on the neck,not caring who was in the room.P that is so disrespectful,dont be doing shit like that in front of your homeboys,and Jayden at that,Tracey scolded P,her face annoyed,feeling that P was disrespecting her,and degrading her in front of guess,and her son.

Tracey pulled away from P,and then headed back to Jayden's side,as Jayden washed out the dish he used.Tell ya moms that chu went over that dude delonte house Jayden,P smiled,his eyes on Jayden.I didn't go over delonte house,i just walked around the block man,Jayden explained.Yea,whatever nigga,P chuckled.We need to have a talk J,come on,Tracey spoke,pulling Jayden towards his bedroom with her.Tracey gently shut Jayden's door as she and Jayden entered.Sit down baby,we need to nip this shit in the bud right here and now,Tracey spoke,sitting herself and Jayden on the bed,her face concerned.Now look,i dont care about chu going over Delonte house,i just dont want chu doing nothing nasty wit him,God created Adam and Eve,not Adam and

Steve,Tracey explained to Jayden in a soft voice.

Ma im not gay,Jayden lied,too afraid to tell Tracey the truth.I had so many of your uncles around you when you was little,aint none of dem touch you,did they? Tracey questioned Jayden.Tracey called the many men she brung around Jayden his uncle,trying to hide the fact that many of them were just random men she slept with.Ma im not stupid,i know dem dudes wasn't my uncles,and they for damn sure wasn't my daddies either,you aint got to lie to me no more ma,i know what's up now,Jayden spoke,two tear drops rolling down his face.I shouldn't have had all dem damn trifling ass men around you,you think that's why you gay,if you are? Tracey questioned Jayden,her face worried.

Naw,im not gay tho,Jayden lied again,a little nervous.None of dem dudes ever touched me,no lie ma,but it's P ma,when you going get rid of that nigga? Jayden spoke,his face saddened and hurt.I know P ya man ma,so im going try and find my own crib soon,im 18,i just cant deal wit that dude no more,Jayden explained,his tears pouring down heavier now.Baby you dont have to leave,look,im going get P ass together real quick,but dont leave yet baby,you still young,it aint easy out there on them streets alone,then you gotta think about bills and all the other shit that comes along wit having your own spot,Tracey spoke,trying to persuade Jayden to stay at home.Jayden was having second thoughts about leaving,and finding his own apartment,but he still wanted to leave home,and quick,away from P,but not his mother Tracey.

Jayden and Tracey talked for another hour,and then headed back into the living area with P and the others.What chall was talkin about,little nigga probably telling you all kinds of bullshit about me,wasn't he? P questioned Tracey,as Tracey ignored him.You betta show P some respect little dude,he the man of the house,you just a rookie baby boy,Lenny spoke to Jayden,his eyes weary from the marijuana he smoked.Lenny leave my motherfucking son alone,Tracey spoke out.Dont pay dem motherfuckers any attention,Tracey whispered to Jayden.

Jayden's anger began to boil over.Lenny shut the fuck up man! Jayden shouted.Tell my moms what went down dawg,tell her motherfucker! Jayden continued to shout,anger in his voice.Little dude take some of that base out cha voice,it aint that motherfucking serious! Lenny spoke to Jayden.Fuck that,tell my ma how you tried to get me to suck ya dick dawg,tell her how you tried to pay me a weak ass fifty dollars to suck ya bitch ass off nigga,only a week after i turned 14 dude! Jayden shouted,unable to keep his anger and secrets locked inside at this point.

I dont know what the fuck you talkin about little nigga?! Lenny lied,guilt covering his face.Lenny what the fuck J talkin about,Lenny i know you aint do some trifling shit like that?! Tracey yelled,grabbing one of P's empty liquor bottles from the dining room table,about to head over to Lenny,to hit him with it.Whoa,whoa,calm down Tracey! P spoke,quickly grabbing Tracey's wrist,forcing her to drop the liquor bottle.Fuck that shit,let me go P! Tracey yelled,squirming back and forth in P's grip.Jayden why the fuck you get cha mother hyped up like that?! P yelled at Jayden.Man fuck you P,you aint shit either dawg! Jayden yelled back at P,at this point he didn't care if P frightened him.Little nigga you asking for a ass whooping now man! P spoke,still holding Tracey in his grasp.

Man im getting the fuck outta here,i see you my man,ya girl and her son some crazy motherfuckers! Lenny spoke to P,heading towards the front door,giving Jayden a nasty look before leaving out,slamming the door behind him.Man,im out too dawg,peace cuz,Trey spoke to P,following behind Lenny,leaving the apartment also.Are you cool now?! P spoke to Tracey,wondering if he should let her go,now that the target of her anger was gone.Im good,but i cant do this shit no more,P you got to go! Tracey spoke,her voice cracking,two tear drops falling from her eyes.Man you going let cha son come inbetween us man,for real tho?! P spoke,his face confused.

P get the fuck out,get out now! Tracey yelled at P,not wanting to hear his voice.If it aint motherfuckers trying fuck my son,it's motherfuckers trying abuse him,get out P,get the fuck out! Tracey screamed,her eyes red and watery.Baby let's talk man,let's talk alright,p spoke,trying to calm Tracey down.Come here baby,let's talk about it,fight that shit,come on,P soothed Tracey,now having his arms around her,guiding her into the bedroom,hoping to change her decision about kicking him out.Tracey wanted P out the house,but another part of her wanted him to stay,tho she knew P was bad for her,and especially Jayden.

Jayden watched P and Tracey go into the bedroom,his face flushed.Jayden went into his bedroom,and then sat there for 30 minutes,until he heard someone knocking at the front door.Jayden headed towards the front door,and then peeped his eye through the peephole,seeing a tall man outside the door.Who is it? Jayden asked the visitor.It's Mike,the visitor answered.

Who you looking for dawg? Jayden questioned Mike.Tracey,or Jayden,i heard they still live around this way,Mike spoke.Jayden unlocked the door,and then opened it,staring Mike in the eyes.What's up dawg,i didn't know you lived in this apartment building,remember me dawg,you had bumped into me just awhile ago on the street,you remember me right man? Mike spoke,his eyes on Jayden.Dont trip little homey,i aint here to rob you or nothing like that dawg,i didn't mean to come over so late either,my bad,but im looking for my people,this chick and her son,they stayed here,her little dude probably grown now tho,Mike explained.

So do a Jayden or Tracey stay here cuz,or this your crib? Mike spoke softly.Dawg im Jayden,and my moms in the other room,Jayden murmured.You motherfucking lying man,Damn man,you grew the fuck up baby boy! Mike spoke,his eyes wide,and his mouth slightly opened.Give me some love man! Mike spoke,wrapping his arms around Jayden,giving Jayden a bearhug.Dawg now that im thinkin about it,you the dude that used to watch me every now and then right? Jayden questioned Mike.Yea,that's me cuz,not on some gay shit,but i got mad love for you little dude,mad love,Mike spoke,his arm now touching Jayden's shoulder.

Tho Jayden knew who Mike was,his memory of Mike was still somewhat blurry.So what's been good wit chu dude? Jayden questioned P.I been chillin man,livin,that's all you can do cuz,what's been good wit chu little homey? Mike spoke,a smile on his face.Mike was excited to see Jayden,even trying hard to keep his tears back,tears of joy.I been cool dawg,just been livin,like you man,Jayden spoke silently,sadness in his eyes.I didn't come at a bad time did i man? Mike questioned Jayden softly.Naw,it's cool,my moms in the other room,i can get her,if you want man? Jayden spoke.Alright man,but im bout to go park my car a little closer to the apartment building cuz,i be back,dont lock the door on my ass man,Mike smiled at Jayden,and then headed out the apartment building.

Jayden shut the front door,but didn't lock it,knowing Mike would soon come back.P headed from the bedroom,and then slowly headed towards Jayden.You tried to play me for a motherfucking fool in front of my homeboys nigga,that was highly disrespectful,P spoke to Jayden,his face frowned.Not now P,Jayden exhaled.Fuck man,tell my moms im bout to leave out for a minute,i dont have time for ya shit right now P,seriously dude,Jayden spoke,stress on his face.Jayden reached for the doorknob of the front door,but was shoved to the floor by P.

Nigga you think you hard?! P shouted at Jayden,as Jayden rested on the floor.Do something motherfucker,buck nigga,buck! P yelled at Jayden,grabbing his belt,and then pulling it from the waist of his pants,wanting to give Jayden another beating with it.Jayden's anger began to swell,he could feel the adrenaline pumping through his body as he thought about all the wicked things P had done to him,he thought about the beatings P gave him,still remembering the sting of P's belt,and then he thought about the hot and wet feeling of P's urine.Jayden caught something hard and glasslike out the corner of his eye as P approached him,it was a liquor bottle.

Im going give you a good ass whooping this time motherfucker,im leaving marks this motherfucking time! P yelled at Jayden,his belt dangling from his hand.P bit his lip,and then pulled his hand back,about to beat Jayden with his belt once again.Jayden reached for the liquor bottle that rested on the floor beside him,the same liquor bottle that Tracey was about to use on P's friend Lenny,he then began to beat P viciously with it,causing P to violently hit the hardwood floor of the apartment,he didn't care if he killed P at that moment,he didn't give P a chance to use his belt at all.

P yelled out in pain as Jayden hammered him with the liquor bottle.Jayden's rage took over him,he continued to strike P in the head with the Liquor bottle,causing the liquor bottle to break into shards,and blood to slowly pour from P's head.P covered his face,trying to avoid the face shots Jayden was giving him.Jayden finally let up,throwing the stub of the broken glass bottle to the floor,his breathing heavy,his heart racing.Jayden felt good,giving P an ass whooping,something he felt P deserved.P held onto his wounded forehead,and then stumbled to his feet again,blood sliding from his wounds,staining his hands,and his shirt.Im going kill you nigga,you got my head leakin and shit,im bout to fuck you up homey,for real,P gasped,still feeling the sting of his wounded head.

P reached for his belt again,and then headed towards Jayden again.Mike entered the house,seeing P heading towards Jayden with his belt.P what the fuck is wrong wit chu man,what chu doing here dawg?! Mike shouted at P.That nigga live here wit me and my moms man! Jayden explained to Mike,backing away from P.That nigga always beating on me,so i smashed his shit! Jayden said proudly.That's alright,im bout to murder this little nigga! P stuttered,heading towards Jayden.It aint happening dawg,you aint touching little dude,you aint touching J man,not while im here motherfucker,not while the fuck im here! Mike shouted in anger,quickly grabbing the belt from P's hand,and then using it to choke P.

What the fuck you doin Mike? P choked out slowly as Mike pulled the belt tighter around his neck,causing him to gasp and wheeze.You said that nigga be beating you,now i want chu to beat him! Mike ordered Jayden,still choking P with his own belt.Jayden stood to his feet,and then headed towards P,his face nervous.I want chu to pull ya motherfucking fist

back and punch this nigga in his shit J!
Mike ordered again.Jayden reached
his hand back,balling it into a hard
fist,and then gave P a swift punch in
the stomach,causing P to gasp in pain
even more.Hit that nigga again J!
Mike ordered Jayden.Jayden bit his
lip,and then gave P another punch in
the stomach,and then another after
that.

Chapter 3

Jayden gave P four more punches to the gut as Mike continued to choke P with the belt,and then backed away from him.Mike loosened and removed the belt from P's neck as P fell to the floor,exhausted and in pain,holding his his stomach with both hands.You had enough motherfucker?! Mike yelled at P as P squirmed around on the floor,still in pain.Here,take your motherfucking belt back nigga! Mike spoke,dropping P's belt right next to him.This shit aint over motherfuckers,ya'll niggas going get got man,im going get both of ya'll fucked up man! P choked out.

Nigga shut the fuck up! Mike shouted,and then spitting on P.P had already gotten a taste of Jayden's revenge,but he had also gotten choked with the very same belt that he used to hurt Jayden with a day ago,karma or not,P was getting back what he had dished out.Tracey entered the living area,her eyes widening as she saw P laying on the hardwood floor,bloodied and beaten,and Mike and Jayden standing above him.What the fuck is going on?! Tracey questioned everyone in the room.Ya man just got his ass beat! Mike smirked at Tracey.Why you got this nigga staying with ya'll Tracey,i thought chu had kicked this nigga to the curve? Mike spoke.Especially after the last time,Mike added.

Mike you cant just be coming up in my motherfucking house causing drama,get the fuck away from P! Tracey yelled,stress covering her face.Causing drama? Mike said,his face confused.This nigga was about to beat on J,your son Tracey,but im causing drama? Mike spoke,his face in disbelief.Jayden dont lie to me,was P about to beat on you? Tracey questioned Jayden softly,her eyes on

Jayden's face.Yea,he was ma,he did it before,Jayden answered Tracey.P we talked in the room,you said you was going cut that shit out?! Tracey yelled at P as P slowly stood to his feet,blood covering sections of his face and clothes.Tracey i love you baby,dont trip off these niggas,P spoke,his voice hoarse.

My dude Jayden musta gave ya little boyfriend a ass whooping before i came in this joint,cause nigga was already leaking blood and shit,Mike spoke to Tracey,a smile on his face.Little J got tired of your shit huh motherfucker? Mike smiled at

P.Man,fuck you cuz! P said to Mike.P this is the last time you going pull some shit like this,get out,Tracey said stiffly,her face blank.Tracey headed into her bedroom,and then began throwing P's clothes and belongings out of her room,kicking them towards him.Get your shit and leave P! Tracey yelled at P as P stood there,dumbfounded.Roll out dawg,get the stepping my dude,Mike smirked at P.Fuck you Tracey,and your motherfucking fatherless son,and i got chu Mike,you know the people i know cuz! P shouted,grabbing his things,and then heading towards the front door,anger on his face.

And you know the people i be motherfucker,i give you my address dawg,1488 Briggs place my nigga,apartment 12,if you about that life,get at me motherfucker,you and whoever,Mike spoke calmly and confident,letting P know that he wasn't afraid of him or the company he kept.Tracey watched P leave with sadness in her eyes.Im out this motherfucker! P shouted as he left the apartment,letting the front door slam behind him.

Come here Baby,Tracey said silently to Jayden.Yea ma,you alright? Jayden questioned Tracey as he approached her.J im sorry i been overlooking the bullshit P was bringing in this house,i thought the nigga could be a father figure to you,your father didn't give two fucks about us,he wasn't shit,so i thought having a man around the house would be good for you,at first i thought P was just trying toughen you up,but i realize that that nigga is just grimey,i mean,Mike was a man in your life growing up,but i think i just wanted a nigga there for me,and just me,and Mike didn't give me that,my dumb ass,i was all about Tracey,i was not ready to be nobody mother,but when i had you i wanted to give you a good upbringing,one that was better than mine,but i kept letting them niggas like P play me for a motherfucking fool,and my stupid ass was their fool,fooling myself into thinking them niggas gave a shit about me or you,Tracey explained to Jayden with tears in her eyes.

P was wrong for the shit he did to you J,and i gotta take some of the blame too,for not setting that nigga straight from the getgo,i was in the wrong too,but i just wanted to say my piece baby,you my child,and i wanna stay in your life,Tracey apologized to Jayden,staring him directly in the eyes.You my mother ma,my love aint going nowhere,Jayden hugged Tracey as Tracey hugged him,both of them silently crying as Mike watched them with approval.

Chapter 4

Two months had passed,and with P gone Jayden had peace at last,he and Mike even picked up where they left off,making up for lost time,their bond just as strong as it was years ago.Little Jayden,you got big on me boy,im still taller than you tho nigga,you was my little dude when you was just a little something,you still is nigga,Mike spoke to Jayden as he and Jayden sat side by side on the sofa playing videogames.Yea man,time flies,im still growing tho man,Jayden spoke,he and Mike's hands still pushing and pulling on their joysticks.I missed you like crazy little homey,but you know how ya moms is,she wanted P bitch ass around,not me,Mike smiled at

Jayden.Yea,i know man,you a cool dude tho Mike,and thank's again dawg,Jayden spoke softly.

Dawg you aint got to keep thanking me for choking out P punk ass,you my little homey,i would blast a motherfucker for you dude,you like my son in some ways,Mike explained to Jayden,his face serious,Mike meant what he said.Much respect dude,Jayden bumped his fist to Mike's.Much respect dawg,Mike bumped his fist to Jayden's.Jayden and Mike continued to play videogames for another hour,still bonding.

Alright little dude,im about to roll out for a couple of days,got some business to take care of outta town,i be back tho,you got my number right J? Mike spoke to Jayden as he rose from the sofa.Yea,i put the joint in my phone,Jayden spoke.Alright,cool,call me up if you got some beef man,seriously dawg,i aint got no problem dealing with a nigga,if they fuck with me or mines,on the real,give me some love before i leave man,Mike spoke to Jayden,awaiting Jayden's embrace.Jayden stood to his feet and then gave Mike a warm hug as they dropped their controllers to the sofa.Mike Gently planted a kiss on Jayden's forehead,and then headed towards the front door,giving Jayden one more glance as his fingers touched the doorknob.

Dont spaz out on the kiss J,i used to give you kisses like that all the time when you was a baby,aint nothing changed,much love,peace out,and tell your moms i said peace,Mike spoke,and then heading out the front door,placing on the bottom lock as he exited the apartment,closing the door softly behind him.Alright man,see you,Jayden spoke before Mike was completely out of the door.Jayden turned off the tv and the videogame console,and then headed to his bedroom,where he placed on his coat and gathered his keys,wanting to take a quick trip to the local corner store.Jayden headed to the corner store,but made a stop at his friend Delonte's house before coming back home.

It was a little after 6:00 pm when Jayden headed back home.Jayden entered the apartment,and then locked the front door behind him,and then placed the bottle of pepsi he brought from the corner store in the fridge,he then headed to Tracey's room afterwards.Ma i got chu a bottle of coke,Jayden spoke silently as he knocked on Tracey's bedroom door,but recieving no answer.Ma you alright in there? Jayden spoke as he slowly cracked Tracey's door open,slowly easing himself into Tracey's room.Jayden saw no signs of Tracey,so he headed back out,closing Tracey's door back,and then heading into his own bedroom.Jayden tossed his coat onto his bed,and then sat at his computer desk,checking his email once turning on his computer.Jayden turned off his computer after awhile,and then stretched himself out on his bed,his arms folded behind his head.

Jayden's cellphone rang,causing him to jump a little.Hello? Jayden spoke as he pulled his phone to his ear,grabbing it from his coat pocket.J this me,im out getting some things for the house,i be back in there a little later,everything alright? Tracey spoke,checking in on Jayden.Everything cool,im just getting back in the house,im just chilling now,Jayden spoke.Alright,well i might call you again when im on my way home,bye baby,Tracey spoke,ending the call.Jayden hung up his phone,and then placed it on his dresser,switching off his lamp,and then leaning back again,his arms to his side,and his eyes staring to the ceiling.Jayden closed his eyes after a few minutes,and then drifted asleep,sleeping for three hours straight,until it was dark out.

Jayden opened his eyes slowly as he awoke,and then turned on his lamp again,checking his clock in the process.Jayden eased himself from his bed,standing to his feet,and then headed into the bathroom,wanting to take a quick shower.The apartment was quiet and empty,only Jayden's footsteps could be heard.Jayden headed to the bathroom,and then began shrugging out of his clothes,starting with his shirt,and then his pants,and then his underwear,until he was completely naked.Jayden then turned on the shower head,and then smoothly stepped into the bathtub,letting the hot water run down his toned body.Jayden heard a silent noise while he showered,but paid the sound no attention as he continued to shower.Jayden stayed in the shower for an hour,until he was done,and then turned off the shower head as he stepped out of the bathtub,his body soaking wet and naked.

Jayden wrapped a short white towel around the waist of his naked body,after using it to dry off first,and then slipped his feet into flip flops as he headed out of the bathroom,steam exiting the bathroom door as he entered the living area.Jayden's eyes widened with shock as he entered the living area,he was now staring P and his homeboys Lenny and Trey in the eyes as they stared back.Dont be looking stupid now little nigga,i told your faggot ass and your fake ass wannabe daddy the shit wasn't over,you thought i was going let some shit like that slide dude,you must be tripping? P spoke calmly to Jayden,his eyes scanning Jayden's practically naked body.You fresh out the shower huh J,the best time to beat a nigga is when he wet or damp,P chuckled sinisterly as Lenny and Trey joined him.

Jayden paused for second,and then began to speak.How you get in here man? Jayden questioned P with a slight stutter,fear overwhelming him.Keys nigga,your moms gave me keys remember homeboy,P said swiftly,his arms crossed as he stood tall,Lenny and Trey sitting on the sofa next to him.Jayden now knew what caused the silent noise he heard when he was in the shower.Dude i dont want no trouble man,just go alright P,let's just squash this beef you got with me man,Jayden pleaded with P softly.Let's squash this beef,P mocked Jayden.Nigga shut your ass up,you aint say that shit when you and Mike was jumping my ass! P shouted.Dawg you treated me like shit since i was a kid,a youngin man,telling me how i wasn't your son,and how my ma shoulda aborted me,then you start beating my ass dawg! Jayden yelled at P,adjusting the towel around his waist.

Man we dont have to have bad blood between us P,we dont dawg,Jayden said silently,trying to get P to listen to reason,but P couldn't care any less,he just wanted to hurt Jayden in some way or form,and that was all he thought about at that moment.Save your begging nigga,you know why im here little nigga,to fuck your whole world up dawg,no damn lie,P smirked at Jayden.I see you gotta little buff,so now you think you hard,P spoke to

Jayden,examining Jayden's body again.Yea,that little nigga put on some muscle,Trey chuckled,as Lenny chuckled along,their eyes on Jayden.Just beat my ass P,you did before,i can take the shit man,if that would make you feel good just do it man,just let me live my life after that man,Jayden said,his eyes glassy,his hands shivering.

The room became silent.Naw nigga,im going mess you up mentally and physically dawg,then me and my homeboys going end your ass,that's what's about to go down little J,P said smoothly as Lenny and Trey stood to their feet,now standing beside P.A cold chill hit Jayden,a twisted and frightening chill,a chill that was caused by Jayden's fear,and the fact that he was naked,and only covered with a towel.Jayden's hands began to twitch as each of the men stared at him,P,Trey,and Lenny.Ya'll going jump me man,just do it,Jayden spoke silently,feeling that a beating was unavoidable at this point.Im going fuck you up mentally first little homey,just chill my nigga,we going deal with chu soon dawg,P said with a sneaky smile.

Go get that nigga,P whispered to Lenny.Jayden flinched,assuming when P said go get that nigga he meant him,but Lenny headed towards the front door instead,silently leaving the apartment.A minute had passed,and Lenny was now reentering the apartment with a beaten up man,a man who's hands were tied together with duck tape,his feet and mouth also.Jayden focused on the mans face,and then realized who the man was after a few seconds,the man was his father,his father Jarrelle.Pops in the house! P snickered,and then turned his gaze back to jayden.Your father going see ya ass get done like the little bitch you are,P spoke to Jayden.Lenny set Jarrelle to his knees,and then turned Jarrelle's head towards Jayden,a smirk on his face.Get your ass on ya knees little nigga! P spoke to Jayden.Jayden hesitated,but eventually let himself fall to his knees as P approached him,P and Trey both.

P pulled down his pants,and then his underwear,and then pushed his exposed crotch towards Jayden's face as tiny tear drops fell from Jayden's eyes.P wanted to shame Jayden in front of his father.Open your mouth nigga,P commanded Jayden silently,his erect penis in his hand.Jayden slowly opened his mouth as the tip of P's penis entered his mouth.Suck that shit nigga! P yelled at Jayden as Jayden began to push his head back and forth on P's manhood.Jarrelle looked away,but Lenny yanked his head back towards the sight of Jayden and P,wanting Jarrelle to witness it.Look at your little son Jarrelle,nigga got better head then his mama,P smiled at Jarrelle as he continued to thrust himself back and forth into jayden's mouth.

Trey unzipped his pants,and then joined in on Jayden and P's physical activities.Deep throat that shit nigga! Trey yelled at Jayden as Jayden swallowed him,and then P again.Make that nigga watch it! P spoke to Lenny,seeing Jarrelle turn his head away from the sight,not wanting to see his son be sexually assualted in front of him,especially by another man,but it was two men instead,that made Jarrelle cringe even more.P and Trey both placed their penises into Jayden's mouth at the same time,causing Jayden to slightly choke.Shit,let me get naked too,Trey spoke out.Trey removed himself from Jayden's mouth,and then began taking off his clothes,as P continued to push in and out of Jayden's mouth.P then took off his shirt,revealing tight abs,and then got himself completely naked,as trey did the same.Trey began sucking on jayden's pecks as he stared over at jarrelle with a smirk on his face.Damn,Tracey taught you well little nigga,P said to Jayden,as he gagged Jayden with his Hard penis.

Everyone jumped for a second as keys entered the front door.Tracey entered the apartment,and her mouth flew open in surprise and shock.Come on Tracey,come join your son baby girl,P smiled at her,while still forcing himself down Jayden's throat.Trey stood to his feet,and then forced Jayden to stroke his penis as he moaned out silently.P im going kill you motherfucker,not my motherfucking son P! Tracey broke into tears,disgust in her face,Tracey was too shocked to do anything at that moment.Turn your head ma,dont watch this shit! Jayden shouted,not wanting his mother to freak out at the sight any longer.Take that bitch clothes off Lenny,P commanded Lenny as Tracey fell to the floor in tears,her hands cuffing into fists,her nails nearly cutting into the flesh of her hands.Lenny began to manhandle Tracey as he pushed Jarrelle to the side.Lenny ripped Tracey's shirt from her body,and then removed her bra,and then forcefully pulling down her pants and panties,as she struggled with the best of her might.

Lenny then placed the naked Tracey on the sofa as he pulled down his pants,shoving his penis into her exposed vagina,groping her naked breast in the process.Ma! Jayden screamed,hearing his mother scream.Shut your ass up nigga,you about to get some dick up in you too! P smacked Jayden with his penis.Jayden began to struggle,but could not overpower P and Trey.Take this shit off nigga! P said,snatching Jayden's towel from his waist,exposing jayden's complete naked body.Easy access nigga,P said as he tossed Jayden's towel to the side.Trey shoved his penis back into Jayden's mouth,and then grabbed the back of Jayden's head,forcing jayden to gag and cough back and forth on his erect penis,until it began to throb intensely.Watch this shit Jarrelle,your son about to get fed dawg! P laughed out as Jarrelle struggled to break free of the tape that kept him in restraint,wanting to kill P if he had the chance.

Trey moaned out as he ejaculated in Jayden's mouth,filling Jayden's mouth with his warm semen.That's what's up Trey,bust all in that faggot nigga mouth! P chuckled.Trey turned Jayden's head towards Jarrelle,showing Jarrelle the semen that slowly dripped from Jayden's lips.Your son the best dawg,Trey smiled at Jarrelle,gently patting Jayden on the head.Jarrelle shook his head with disappointment and fury as he made eye contact with the tearful eyed Jayden.That's beautiful right there,P smiled,referring to the semen that covered Jayden's lips.Get that ass in doggystyle nigga,P ordered Jayden as he held onto Jayden's arm.

Another tear drop slid down Jayden's face.

This nigga over here crying,pussy ass nigga,Trey spoke,seeing the tear drops fall from Jayden's eyes.Jayden gagged,not wanting Trey's semen in his mouth.Swallow that shit nigga! Trey ordered Jayden as P bent Jayden over,placing Jayden's face against the hard floor,and then placing himself behind him.Im going bust ya motherfucking head open if you dont swallow that shit little nigga! Trey yelled at Jayden as Jayden slowly let Trey's semen travel down his throat,his face stiff and saddened.P entered into Jayden's cavity,and then began thrusting himself back and forth into Jayden as Jayden whimpered and whined the entire time.Shut the fuck up nigga,you aint tough now dawg! P shouted at Jayden,latching his hands around the back of Jayden's neck as he continued to pound Jayden's posterior with force.

Jayden tried to imagine that he was somewhere else,but he could still feel P inside him,P's grunts and moans whisking against his ear.Jayden could see the sofa rock,knowing that Tracey was being tooken advantage of just as well as he was,but Jayden could only focus on the pain he felt at the moment,having P's penis stroke back and forth inside of him.Trey placed his penis back into Jayden's mouth as

P continued to forcefully enter himself into Jayden,speeding up and then slowing down.Aw shit! P Shouted,shooting himself into Jayden.Jayden could feel P's hot semen flood into him.Fuck you dawg! Jayden screamed at P.Naw,i fucked you nigga! P snickered,pulling himself out of Jayden,and then smacking Jayden on his behind.

P set Jayden on his knees again,as he and Trey surrounded Jayden.Jayden could now hear Tracey being punched viciously by Lenny as she screamed out in pain.Leave my fucking moms outta this! Jayden yelled in anger,now hearing a blood gurgling sound escaping Tracey's lips,until the sound eventually disappeared.Lenny stood to his feet again as he pulled up his pants,his hands covered in blood,Tracey's blood.Dawg im going fucking kill you man! Jayden yelled out,now consumed by rage.Jayden began to struggle,almost escaping P and Trey's grip,but he still wasn't strong enough.Lenny gave Jayden a smug smile as he moved closer to him,caressing Jayden's face,while Jayden began to spit at him,anger in his eyes.I should make you suck my dick too,so you can taste ya mothers pussy,Lenny said to Jayden,and then heading in the other direction.

Round two little nigga! P spoke to Jayden,a smirk on his face.Lenny grabbed Jarrelle,and then brung him closer to Jayden,p,and Trey,wanting Jarrelle to see the trio in action.Watch it nigga! Lenny whispered into Jarrelle's ear as the naked P and Trey towered over the naked Jayden,masturbating themselves,but keeping Jayden's arms locked in the grip of their free hands,the ones they didn't use to masturbate with.Jayden closed his eyes,hoping everything would be over soon,as P and Trey continued to stroke themselves over him.Here we go,watch it Jarrelle,P said to Jayden's father,feeling himself about to climax,and wanting Jarrelle to see it with his own eyes.Ah! Fuck man,im about to bust in your son face! P shouted as he and Trey ejaculated all over Jayden's nude body,starting with his face.

Jayden kept his eyes shut and his mouth closed,not wanting anymore of P or Trey's semen inside of him.Bitch ass nigga! P grunted in pleasure as he squirted another round of semen into Jayden's face.Pussy ass nigga,Trey moaned silently,brushing the wet and semen covered tip of his erect penis onto Jayden's face.Tho Jarrelle wasn't the best father in the world,he couldn't bare to see his son Jayden in this position,watching P and Trey's semen slowly slide down Jayden's face and chin,falling onto his pecks,and then running down his exposed abdomen.Damn,that was a good nut,Trey exhaled,still holding his penis in his hand.You had blood running down my face nigga,now you got cum running down yours,P said to

Jayden in a clear voice.We just gave your son a bath dawg,you should be happy nigga! P laughed out sarcastically as Trey and Lenny chuckled along with him.

P,Lenny,and Trey were all abusive and perverse men,men who got thrills outta sexually humiliating and abusing other people,regardless of the persons gender.Lenny pushed Jarrelle to the side as P and Trey shrugged back into their clothes,finally letting go of Jayden's arms,letting him free.Jayden quickly grabbed his towel,and then used it to wipe P and Trey's semen from his body as they laughed at him,feeling proud of what they had done to him.Jayden was about to head over to Tracey,but was kicked in the side by P before he could do anything.Jayden fell to the floor after being kicked by P,and then began holding his side,feeling the sting of P's sneakers against his bare skin.How you like being my woman nigga? P smiled at Jayden,making light of the fact that he had sexually assualted Jayden.

Fuck you P,just kill me or just go now man! Jayden said in a strained voice.P kneeled to his knees,and then swiftly and roughly grabbed Jayden by the head,staring Jayden directly in the eyes,his hands pressing against each side of Jayden's cheeks.Nigga i remember when you used to want me to pick ya pussy ass up when you was a baby,when that nigga mike wasn't around to hold and spoil ya bitch ass,he wasn't around this time either,nigga always trying save ya pussy ass,he aint save you this time,shit,nigga after all the cum i put up in you you might as well say im ya daddy now,you got a part of me in you now nigga,i was going bust a cap in ya ass,but now i want chu to live nigga,knowing that chu got got dawg,everytime ya little faggot ass boyfriend fuck you i want chu to think about me nigga,im in ya dome now man,P smirked,wanting to toy with Jayden's mind.

P then stood back up to his feet,releasing Jayden's face from his strong grip,and then headed to the front door as Trey and Lenny followed behind him.We out nigga,P smirked at Jayden one last time,and then exited the front door with Trey and Lenny behind him,leaving Jayden naked and silent on the hardwood floor of the apartment.Jayden felt used and degraded,but angry too,feeling he was powerless to stop P and the others.Jayden slammed his fist into his hand,angry and highly upset,his face flushed.Jarrelle began to move and tussle around,wanting Jayden to notice him,so that Jayden could free him.Jayden quickly removed the duck tape from Jarrelle's legs and arms,and then his mouth,using scissors to do it.Jarrelle pushed Jayden out of the way as soon as he was released,and then quickly headed towards the window,quickly lifting it.

P and the others were sliding themselves into a ford sedan when Jarrelle spotted them.Jarrelle quickly reached into his jeans,pulling a gun from the gunstrap around his thigh,and then began shooting at P and his homeboys out the window,causing them to panic and quickly pull off,firing a couple of rounds themselves before leaving.Oh my lawd! Jayden heard his neighbor Ms Glenda scream as she heard the gunshots,even tho she was used to it.Jayden could also hear the sound of screeching tires as P and the others blasted off down the street.You alright Jarrelle? Jayden spoke,calling Jarrelle by his name instead of calling him dad.Dad? Jayden questioned Jarrelle again,calling him dad this time,hoping Jarrelle would answer.Nigga im not your dad,i dont produce faggots,them niggas told me about chu,who is this nigga delonte? Jarrelle spoke,his face fuming with anger as he stared at the naked and blank faced jayden.

Nigga you put yourself in this shit,do you know what some people do to faggots,gumps? Jarrelle spoke to Jayden,placing his gun back into his pants,and then placing his shirt over his pants.Dad? Jayden said,his face hurt and saddened.Your lifestyle got chu into this shit nigga,and ya moms hoe ass to blame too,fucking every Tom and Harry,dont know what type of nigga she fucking,Jarrelle said with a mean mug,his eyes on Jayden.I care for you dawg,but im not accepting that lifestyle you living,in some ways P aint wrong,but that nigga aint fucking with me or my blood,Jarrelle explained to Jayden,causing small tears to exit Jayden's eyes.Man the fuck up nigga! Jarrelle yelled at Jayden.Man so what if i like dudes,that nigga aint have no right doing what the fuck he did man! Jayden shouted at Jarrelle,finally admitting that he was same sex oriented,his face angered.

Nigga who is you talking to,you must have forgot that i was your father dude? Jarrelle said in a stern voice,moving closer to Jayden.Jayden became silent as Jarrelle approached him.Jarrelle gave Jayden a mean glare,and then swiftly punched Jayden in the jaw,causing Jayden to stumble slightly.Jayden held his jaw,and then gave his father a frown.You wanna try me nigga? Jarrelle questioned Jayden,seeing the frown on Jayden's face.You my pops man,i respect you,Jayden said silently,and then turning away from Jarrelle.Jarrelle headed towards the front door,and then gave Jayden a stare.Lock up the house,and dont tell the feds shit,i aint got snitches in my family,i wanna handle these niggas myself,Jarrelle spoke to Jayden,and then leaving out the apartment.

Jayden had almost forgotten about Tracey,too angry to think straight,thinking about P and the others,and his father,who wasn't a father to him at all.Jayden quickly ran over to Tracey,seeing her face bloodied and beaten,her face puffy,her eyes closed shut.Jayden immediately panicked,assuming the worst.Ma wake up! Jayden said repeatly,tears streaming down his face,lightly falling onto Tracey's nude body.Tracey didn't respond to Jayden at all,no matter how hard he shook or shouted at her to wake up.Jayden placed his hands over his forehead afterwards,deeply stressed and grief stricken.Jayden looked over at the telephone that sat on the coffee table,wanting to call the police,if it meant helping Tracey,regardless of what his father Jarrelle had told him.

Jayden headed towards the telephone,completely ignoring what Jarrelle had said,he just wanted to help Tracey,that's all he wanted.The telephone rang just as Jayden was about to pick it up,causing Jayden to flinch slightly.Hello?! Jayden answered the phone quickly.What's up,this Mike J,everything cool over there man? Mike said calmly,waiting for Jayden to reply.Yea,i gotta hit chu up a little later tho man,Jayden said,his voice unsteady.You sure everything cool dawg? Mike questioned Jayden again,concern in his voice.Yea man,everything cool,gotta go tho man,Jayden said,trying his best to rush Mike off of the phone,so that he could call the police like he intended.

Jayden dont lie to me dawg,you sure everything is cool,i aint leave town yet man,im still around the way,i can be there in a minute J,did something go down,you need me to fuck a nigga up? Mike spoke.Man,P and em came pass the house and did some fucked up shit to me and my moms,shit that im not even going discuss on the phone man,them niggas gone now tho,Jayden spoke to Mike,hurt in his voice.Man i be there little dude! Mike spoke,ending the call quickly before Jayden could say anything else.Jayden placed the telephone back on the hook,forgetting to call the police,but instead headed into Tracey's room for a blanket,using it to cover Tracey's exposed body.Jayden could hear someone heading up the apartment buildings staircase,and then Mike quickly entered into the apartment through the front door,his face worried.

Jayden quickly called an ambulance for the unconscious Tracey,and then turned his gaze back towards Mike.Jayden then slightly slid the cover back,showing only Tracey's bruised face to Mike as Mike watched silently.Tsk,Mike said with disappoinment,after witnessing Tracey's face.You alright dawg?! Mike questioned Jayden quickly,and then his eyes focused on Jayden's nude body.What the fuck them niggas do man,why you naked?! Mike spoke,his eyes scanning Jayden,and his voice cracking just a little.Them niggas did what they did,Jayden said silently to Mike,not staring Mike in the eyes.Naw J,tell me what them niggas did man?! Mike spoke,now kneeling down,wanting to meet Jayden's stare.Look at me J,Mike ordered Jayden in a stern voice.Jayden rose his head,now meeting Mike's worried face.

Man i like dudes,im gay nigga,im gay Mike,and P been fucking with me ever since man,that nigga always treated me like shit,but once that nigga found out i like dudes that shit got worse man,that's the reason why he was about to fuck me up the last time,then when we kicked his ass that nigga wanted me and ya ass six feet under man,Jayden explained to Mike.That nigga and his homeboys did me and my moms dirty,they did us Mike,Jayden said with anger.They did ya'll,i know you aint trying tell me them niggas raped you,tell me the truth J,that shit dont make you any less of a person or a man J,did them niggas put they thing in you man,give me a straight answer man? Mike spoke softly to Jayden,hoping Jayden would give him an answer.Yea man,Jayden answered Mike hesitantly,feeling slightly embarrassed to say the words.

Fuck man! Mike shouted after recieving Jayden's news,punching the sofa,wanting to release his anger on something.Listen J,ya business is ya business man,so what if you like niggas,i like pussy,i even got head from another nigga before,i aint going lie,i dont give a fuck about chu liking other dudes,and you liking dudes dont make P ass in the right,that nigga still wrong as fuck,for real,Mike explained to Jayden.You thought i was going look at chu differently if i found out the root of the shit between you and P,huh J,answer me little dude? Mike spoke,his eyes on Jayden.Yea man,you got niggas out here beating the fuck outta niggas for being out with their gay shit,you even got niggas killing gay dudes,then you got the no homo shit,niggas dont wanna be bothered with chu no more after they find out chu swing like that man,Jayden explained to Mike,anger in his voice.

My pops was here,they made that nigga watch me get violated,And even that nigga disowned me for liking dudes man,but i dont give a fuck,that nigga was barely in my life anyway,Jayden spoke.I dont need no nigga in my life,no fucking body dawg,Jayden lied,his voice cracking,his eyes watery.Nigga you hurting man,im not stupid J,come

here little homey,you aint too grown
for me to hold you nigga,bring ya ass
over here dawg,Mike spoke,grabbing
Jayden into his big arms,tightly
holding Jayden in his warm embrace
as tears poured down Jayden's face.

Let that shit out man,let that shit out
J,i aint going nowhere dawg,nigga i
watched ya ass grow from a boy into
a man dawg,i aint going nowhere
man,that's my motherfucking word
dawg,and them niggas,P,and them
fools he be rolling with all going get
smoked,i dont like talking about guns
and about killing motherfuckers
around you J,but them niggas gotta

get popped man,im fucking
sorry,man,me just thinking about
how i used to hold you when you was
a baby,and now to hear about a nigga
beating you and motherfucking
raping you,i aint letting that shit
slide,it aint happening J,Mike said in a
stern voice,tears now slowly pouring
from his eyes as well,tho he didn't
want Jayden to see them,wanting to
keep his tough guy image,which he
was,but with a touch of
gentleness.Jayden and Mike could
now hear the sound of ambulance
sirens as they continued to embrace
tightly.

Chapter 5

The ambulance had arrived for Tracey.Jayden and Mike pulled Tracey back into her clothes as she still sat silently and motionless on the sofa.Jayden then got himself dressed,as Mike opened the front door for the paramedics.Tracey was then placed onto a stretcher as the paramedics carried her down the stairs of the apartment building,and then loading her into the ambulance as Jayden and Mike watched.Jayden and Mike followed behind the ambulance,and then headed up to the emergency room with Tracey once they arrived at the hospital.

Jayden had tears falling from his eyes as Mike gently pat him on the back,trying to soothe his anguish.The doctors advised Jayden and Mike to wait in the other room as they tried to revive Tracey.Mike placed his hand on Jayden's shoulder as they both took a seat in one of the hospital chairs.Ya moms going be alright J,she a fighter man,everything going be cool,Mike comforted Jayden as

Jayden sat very quietly,his face blank.The hours passed,and it was soon morning.Jayden and Mike had spent the night at the hospital.The sunrays shined through the windows as Jayden awoke,his eyes weary.Mike slept in the chair beside Jayden,his eyes shut,his head leaned to the side.Good morning,a male voice spoke,causing Jayden to flinch and Mike to awaken.Good morning,both Jayden and Mike replied to the man.Im doctor Thomas,your mother is in stable condition,but we still want to keep her for a couple of days,just as a precaution,she suffered multiple blows to her head and face,and she had a severe concussion when she was first brought in,but she's a little better now,the man spoke.

Even tho your mother is recovering,she unfortunately lost her baby,your little brother or sister,the fetus died three weeks ago,so it wasn't caused by the incident that happened to you and her,she passed it last night,sorry,doctor Thomas said silently.Tracey had no clue that she was pregnant with P's child or that she miscarried it,that just added more fuels to the already blazing fire.We understand that you and your mother both were sexually assualted,i think it would be a good idea if you had yourself examined too,and we also have mental care classes available,free of charge,we understand that things like this can cause victims stress and anxiety,and sometimes longterm effects on a persons mental structure,doctor Thomas explained to Jayden,his voice soft and apologetic.Naw,no thank's,im cool,Jayden replied to doctor Thomas,his face stiff.

You may come and see your mother if you want,she's sedated at the moment,but she can have visitors now,family only,doctor Thomas spoke,guiding Jayden and Mike towards Tracey's room.Is he,is he a relative or spouse? doctor Thomas questioned Jayden softly,wanting to know if Mike had any relation with Tracey before entering her hospital room.He a friend of the family,he knew my mother since before i was born,he like family to me man,he cool,Jayden explained to doctor Thomas.Alright,it's fine,doctor Thomas said softly,a thin smile on his face.Doctor Thomas guided Jayden and Mike into Tracey's hospital room,checking her one last time before leaving her alone with Jayden and Mike.Jayden rested his head on Tracey's chest,and then gave her a quick and gentle kiss on the cheek,examining the dark reddish purplish bruises on her swollen face as she slumbered.

Let's go back to the crib,this shit going fuck with ya head J,Tracey be alright man,we be back to pick her up,Mike spoke softly to Jayden,gently placing his arm around Jayden's shoulder as he guided him back out the room,silently shutting the door.We be back in a few days,just let us know when ya'll releasing her,i dont want my little homeboy to see his moms like that,Mike explained to doctor Thomas.Sure thing,we'll keep the two of you updated on her status,doctor Thomas waved at Jayden and Mike as they exited the hospital.Give me the word J,we can blast P and em other niggas tonight or tomorrow,either way them niggas getting dealt with,it's up to you baby boy? Mike said once he and Jayden entered the car,hoping to end Jayden's grief by ending P and his homeboys lives.Mike studied Jayden's face,waiting for Jayden to give him an answer.Jayden hesitated to answer Mike,but then a frown grew on his face as he opened his mouth to speak.

Kill them niggas,kill all dem motherfuckers man,Jayden said calmly,finally speaking,and then began to silently stare out the window of the car.I got chu J,we taking em niggas out tonight man,we going stop pass my place first,get some heat,then we going pick up my boy Derrick a little later,Mike explained to Jayden as they pulled off.Mike drove to his place,and then neatly packed a black trash bag full of guns into the back of his trunk,and then driving himself and Jayden back to Jayden and Tracey's place,where he taught Jayden the basics about guns and how they worked.I wanna take these niggas out myself J,me and my homeboy Derrick going deal with these niggas,but i want chu to kill P's ass personally,now i know you probably aint about that life,and i hate that im telling you this shit J,but that shit would make me feel so much motherfucking better if you popped that nigga yourself,for all the shit that nigga then done to you,Mike explained carefully to Jayden.

Im going fuck P up first,and then i want chu to load that nigga J,Mike said to Jayden,his face serious.You going do it or you want me to finish the nigga? Mike questioned Jayden as Jayden sat silently.Jayden pondered to himself for a minute,tho he wasn't a killer,he wanted P to pay for his crimes,but a part of him didn't want to take a life,but he would have to make a choice when the time arrived,when he was staring P face to face.

Listen J,i know this shit aint ya thing,so let's just get fucked up tonight instead,get some drinks in our system,and then we can get them niggas tomorrow,Mike spoke,seeing that Jayden was hesitant to answer his question about who would take P's life,knowing that Jayden wasn't a killer.Jayden smiled at Mike,and then began to chuckle as Mike began to playfully wrestle him on the sofa.Ya bitch ass,i tried to teach you how to fight when you was little,and you still cant fight worth a damn nigga,Mike snickered as he towered over Jayden,giving Jayden playful and gentle blows to the chest as Jayden and he chuckled deeply.Mike then pulled himself from Jayden,sitting himself up on the sofa,his smile fading.

Come here J,i wanna holla at chu for a minute dawg,Mike said softly,his face serious.What's up? Jayden spoke as he rose himself up,wondering what is was that Mike wanted to tell him.Come here nigga,Mike said to Jayden again,his legs gapped and his arm hanging across the sofa.Jayden moved closer to Mike,clueless to what Mike wanted.Bring ya ass here dawg,Mike chuckled,yanking Jayden into his left arm,curving it around Jayden's shoulders.You know i used to have a thing for ya moms,man she was banging dawg,she still is,but me and her never went down that road man,but nigga i loved you dawg,from the moment ya mama had you i loved ya little ass nigga,that was the only reason i stuck around ya moms for so long,nigga you was a cute little something,you had them little puppy dog eyes,you still got them nigga,Mike snickered as he held Jayden even tighter to him.

Let me know if im bothering you dawg,talking about how sexy ya moms was,i know some niggas just deal with the kids because they want a piece of the moms,but i wanted you and ya moms nigga,you was my little dude,i woulda raised you myself if i could,but ya moms start tripping,dont get it twisted J,i wasn't on no pedophile shit,i dont want chu to think i was trying pluck ya little baby cherry or some shit like that,but i loved you man,i still fucking love you,it's like you changed me man,back in the day i woulda been smoked P's ass man,but chu softened my ass up J,Mike spoke silently to Jayden,still holding Jayden tightly as Jayden listened carefully to his words.You probably dont love my ass like you used to,you grew up on my ass,Mike smiled thinly at Jayden.Naw,you a cool dude Mike,i respect you dawg,and i do love you man,dont spaz out man,my bad,im not trying turn you gay or nothing like that,Jayden spoke,flinching just a little as he spoke the words,thinking Mike might hit him for saying something tender to him,something some would consider gay,not knowing any better,thinking that only gay men could show affection to each other.

What chu tripping for J,that shit actually made my day man,you only get a few motherfuckers in this world who love you and respect you man,i respect and appreciate that shit little dude,honestly,Mike said with conviction.You still little J to me,but big J at the same time,Mike chuckled as he softly kissed Jayden on the forehead.Dont get pissed off at me Jayden,but i got a question for you little dude? Mike smiled softly,his eyes on Jayden.Go ahead dawg,Jayden insisted.I know you like dudes and all,but how do ya father and other niggas that chu related to make you feel man,even me? Mike questioned Jayden,waiting silently for Jayden to reply.Jayden snickered softly to Mike's question,and then began to speak.The same way you feel about your mother and ya sisters,they women,and you like women right,Jayden explained to Mike,a smile on his face.Even tho ya mother and ya sisters are women,im pretty sure you dont look at them in the same way you look at ya girlfriend or wife dude,it's the same thing with us gay dudes,Jayden furthered explained to Mike,as Mike listened carefully with enthusiasm.

Yea,i feel you little dude,but i got some sexy ass motherfucking female cousins i would smash,if they wasn't family,Mike chuckled deeply in his deep voice as Jayden joined him.I mean,i got a hard on when i saw my moms naked,i was like 6 or 7 tho,i was a young buck,at that age you get a hard on to just about any motherfucking thing,i thank God i dont think shit like that no more tho,Mike snickered as Jayden broke into laughter.If you was to see ya male cousin or me naked,would that shit get chu hard dawg,tell the truth dawg,i aint going try and beat ya ass or nothing like that,just keep it real J,tell me nigga? Mike smirked at Jayden as Jayden blushed on the inside.Man you wrong as shit for asking me a question like that Mike,but im going give you a honest and straight answer man,Jayden chuckled.

Man i look at my couins as family,but my cousin Lonzo aint that bad looking,but i dont wanna fuck him,us gay dudes dont wanna fuck every dude we see,like im pretty sure ya'll straight dudes dont wanna bang every girl ya'll see,you on the other hand,you like a mentor or father figure to me man,but at the same time,you aint my real pops,this shit making me feel weird now man,Jayden spoke to Mike,giving Mike something to think about.True,and i feel you on that not wanting to fuck every chick i see man,cause that bitch Tammy that live downstairs from me is ugly as a motherfucker,i would have to fuck that broad with a bag on her head,Mike snickered as Jayden snickered along.Im trying get fucked up now,im about to go to the corner store right quick,i be back,Mike spoke to Jayden,standing to his feet,and then heading towards the front door as Jayden continued to sit on the sofa.Alright,im going leave the door unlocked,Jayden said to Mike as Mike left the apartment.

Mike headed to the corner store for a bottle of liquor,and then headed back to Jayden's place.Mike entered the apartment,shutting and locking the door behind him,and then headed towards the sofa,sitting himself beside Jayden,and then pulling a brown paper bag covered bottle of liquor from his coat pocket,sitting it on the coffe table in front of Him and Jayden,grabbing a pack of plastic cups from his coat pockets also.Mike took the bottle of liquor out of the bag,twisting off the lid,and then poured he and Jayden a cup of liquor,filling both of their cups halfway,but not to the top.Drink nigga,Mike ordered Jayden as Jayden placed the cup of liquor to his lips,taking just a sip.Mike smiled at Jayden,and then took a sip of his own liquor,taking small sips at first,but then swallowing down all the liquor at once.Nigga i forgot chu wasn't legal to drink,but i wont tell if you wont nigga,Mike snickered as Jayden took another sip of liquor from the cup.

Jayden could feel the liquor heating through his body as he continued to drink.Mike took off his coat and then leaned back,pulling Jayden even closer to him.Mike reached for the bottle of liquor after finishing his cup of liquor.Jayden wasn't much of a drinker,he had placed his still slightly filled cup of liquor on the table.Mike pushed the bottle of liquor to his lips and then began to sip,but then slowly placed the bottle towards Jayden's lips,wanting Jayden to take a sip.Naw,no thank's dawg,im good now,Jayden chuckled silently,not wanting anymore liquor.Just take another sip nigga,Mike smirked,still holding the liquor bottle towards

Jayden's lips.Alright man,Jayden smiled as he opened his mouth,allowing Mike to slowly pour the liquor down his throat.Nigga i used to feed you bottles,now im feeding you liquor,Mike snickered as he twirled the bottle around in Jayden's mouth,wanting to make sure Jayden got drunk,hoping it would ease Jayden's nerves,and take his mind off his pain.

Mike then placed the bottle back into his mouth,taking a few more sips,and then placing it back on the table.I love you nigga,Mike smiled at Jayden,tightly holding Jayden in his grasp as he and Jayden both sat on the sofa pissy drunk now.Nigga you my dawg man,i love too man,Jayden snickered,his eyes weary.I love you more tho little nigga,Mike snickered back at Jayden,giving Jayden a kiss on the forehead,and then easing a kiss on Jayden's lips,and then his cheek.Nigga im about to take a shower,you then got me messed up Mike,Jayden smirked at Mike as he stumbled to the bathroom,pulling off some of his clothes as he entered.Mike stretched himself out on the sofa,and then eventually fell asleep,while Jayden showered in the bathroom.Jayden let the soap and water run down his naked body,thoroughly washing himself,remembering that he hadn't since the night he was sexually assualted by P and Trey.

Jayden reached his hand towards the towel rack after he was finished with his long shower,grabbing a short white towel from the rack,pulling it around his waist,and then stepping his wet feet into a pair of shower shoes as he headed out the bathroom.Mike had awoken around the time Jayden was done with his shower,and was now sober.Come over here J! Mike called out to Jayden as Jayden was about to enter his bedroom,wanting to dry himself off,and place himself into clean clothes.Alright man,let me get dressed first dawg,Jayden spoke to Mike.Naw,come here little dude,Mike spoke again,not caring that Jayden was soaking wet and only in a towel.Yea,what's good Mike? Jayden said softly,his eyes on Mike.I wanna make sure you cool and everything,so can i spend the night dawg? Mike spoke to Jayden,his eyes now studying Jayden's physique.Yea man,of course you can man,Jayden said swiftly,without hesitation.Alright,cool man,you then really grew on my ass little nigga,damn nigga,you got pecks and shit,abs,damn little dude,Mike chuckled,studying Jayden from head to toe.

I need to take a quick shower my damn self,is that cool? Mike spoke to Jayden.Yea man,make yourself at home dawg,it's towels on the rack,Jayden said to Mike,and then headed into his bedroom.Mike shrugged out of his clothes as he entered the bathroom.Jayden could hear Mike turn on the showerhead just as he entered his bedroom,he could also hear his cellphone ringing and vibrating on his bed.Jayden dried his hands on the towel he wore around his waist,and then quickly picked up his phone,placing it to his ear.Hello,what's up? Jayden said smoothly and swiftly,answering his phone.This Delonte,i aint seen you in awhile man,Delonte spoke.I aint seen you in awhile either man,Jayden spoke back.Jayden and Delonte spoke for nearly fifteen minutes,and then finally ended their call.Jayden didn't have time to place on any clothes or to dry off,becoming distracted by he and Delonte's phone call.Where you at J,you got any deodorant around this joint?! Jayden could hear Mike speak.

Jayden adjusted the towel around his waist and then headed out into the living area,spotting Mike pratically naked,soaking wet,and only covered with a towel,just as he was.Jayden's eyes widened as he examined Mike's strong and built physique,seeing the bulging muscles in Mike's arms,and the hard pecks on Mike's chest.Jayden felt slightly nervous.I got deodorant in my room,my moms got some too,but she got that dove and shit,i got some axe,and i got a brand new stick of degree in my room,Jayden explained,his face nervous.Nigga you all nervous and shit,i then seen you naked before,you seen me too,you probably too young to remember tho,Mike smiled at Jayden.We both got the same thing,aint nothing to be shy about man,Mike smiled softly at Jayden as Jayden slightly smiled back.

Mike's phone rung,startling him and Jayden.Hello?! Mike spoke as he pulled his phone to his ear,grabbing it out of his coat pocket.Mike's face switched from facial expression to facial expression as he listened carefully to the person on his phone.Wait J! Mike spoke,seeing Jayden about to go back into his bedroom.Alright man,Mike said to his caller as he hung up his phone,and then turned his gaze towards Jayden.Mike's friend Derrick had called him.My homeboy Derrick said P's homeboy Trey just got capped out,the nigga dead,got shot ten times man,dude gone,Mike explained to Jayden as Jayden's mouth flew open.Damn,are you serious dawg? Jayden whispered to Mike.Hell yea man,Mike said silently to Jayden.A part of jayden was shocked,but another part of him was in some ways relieved about Trey's death.Jayden and Mike quickly turned to the front door,hearing loud thumps against it,someone was knocking,and knocking loud.

Jayden peeped his eye through the peephole,and then slightly opened the door,seeing who it was,it was Jarrelle.Hey pops,Jayden said stiffly,his eyes on Jarrelle.Ya heard yet? Jarrelle said to Jayden.Huh,heard what? Jayden said,not knowing what his father meant.That nigga Trey,i blasted his motherfucking ass! Jarrelle said proudly,his eyes on Jayden.Jayden now knew who had killed Trey,it was jarrelle.Damn pop,i thought chu was just talking shit when you said you was going handle them man,Jayden said with surprise in his voice.Ya damn right,i capped that nigga out,made his ass cry like a bitch first,Jarrelle chuckled,proud of his handiwork.You just getting out the shower or something? Jarrelle spoke to Jayden,and then peeping his eyes through the crack of the front door,spotting Mike,and then looking back at Jayden again,his face frowned.What the fuck is going on up in that motherfucker?! Jarrelle yelled at Jayden,causing Jayden to flinch.

Ya'll niggas took a shower together or something,why both of ya'll niggas naked in towels Jayden,you better give me a motherfucking straight answer Jayden?! Jarrelle shouted again,his nostrils flaring.Dad it aint like that man,Jayden quickly spoke,trying to explain himself to Jarrelle,knowing that Jarrelle thought that he and Mike had done something intimate with each other.You outta my life nigga,keep being a niggas woman Jayden,keep allowing yourself to be some mans motherfucking cum dumpster you faggot ass nigga! Jarrelle yelled at Jayden,his anger boiling,him seeing Jayden and another man pratically naked in the same house together.Pops,my moms fighting for her life,and you doing this to me man,i need you nigga! Jayden cried out to jarrelle.Save them motherfucking tears Jayden! Jarrelle yelled.Mike eased himself behind Jayden,and then began to nibble on Jayden's ear,in front of Jarrelle,knowing he was pissing Jarrelle off even more.

Im outta this motherfucker,fuck you and him! Jarrelle shouted,and then heading back down the apartment buildings staircase,slamming the door violently behind him,causing the sound of the slamming door to echoe throughout the building.Jayden gently closed the front door and then turned around towards Mike,hurt in his face.Mike reached his hand pass Jayden,locking the front door,and then pulling Jayden towards him softly.My bad man,i pissed ya pops off even more,i was wrong for that,but i know that nigga do care about chu dawg,Mike spoke softly to

Jayden.Im not trying be on some gay shit,but you need a mans touch dawg,ya father aint trying give it to you,but i want to J,Mike said softly to Jayden,pushing his lips gently to Jayden's as their chests,towels,and thighs met.Did it feel good man? Mike questioned Jayden silently,wanting to know if Jayden enjoyed the kiss.Jayden hesitated to answer,but finally said something.

Yea,it did man,Jayden said nervously to Mike,not wanting to stare Mike in the eyes.Look at me J,Mike spoke gently,giving Jayden another gentle kiss on the lips as he and Jayden's eyes met.Mike's breathing became heavy as he rushed his lips into Jayden's again,and again after that.Damn man,i knew you since you was a little boy man,i cant be feeling this way about chu J,fuck man,Mike spoke,his voice shaky.Mike pulled away from Jayden,but Jayden pulled him back,now finishing what Mike started.Man im like a father to you man,chill on that shit J,Mike stuttered,trying to resist Jayden's lips with all his might,but he couldn't,his attraction for Jayden had grown too strong at this point,and them being pratically naked didn't help any.Mike began kissing Jayden back,as their hearts pounded against their chests.Mike began kissing jayden with even more passion,even bringing his tongue out to play.

Nigga im not going violate chu like this dawg,i held you as a baby nigga,why you doing this shit to me J? Mike muttered as he and Jayden continued to kiss.Mike felt guilty about what he and Jayden were doing,but he was overtaken by lust,lust for a young man he knew his entire life,a young man he watched develope from a boy into an attractive young man.

J chill alright,come on man,let's chill on this shit man,Mike exhaled deeply as he and Jayden's lips separated.Why dawg? We grown man,Jayden spoke to Mike,catching his breath in the process.Because im old enough to be ya father little dude,nigga i watched you grow up man,that's why,Mike spoke,his eyes meeting Jayden's gaze.So what nigga,im a grown ass man now,i know what i want outta life dawg,you aint putting a fucking gun to my head man,let's do what we do,Jayden spoke,not wanting to stop his kissing session with Mike.Man this shit aint right dawg,niggas know you was my little dude when you was little dawg,now they going think i been fucking you since day one J,that aint a cool image man,niggas going be trying clown me and shit,Mike explained,his face pained.

Fuck them man,we both grown Mike,what we doing aint none of their damn business man,aint nobody here but chu and me,so aint nobody telling shit,Jayden spoke,his eyes locked on Mike.This shit aint cool Jayden,im about to put my clothes back on and chill on the couch dawg,Mike explained to Jayden as he began to turn the other way,away from Jayden.Jayden grabbed Mike's arm as Mike turned away from him,pulling Mike back towards him.You acting like a pussy ass nigga now Mike,you was supposed to be big Mike,act like it nigga,Jayden spoke to Mike,wanting to provoke Mike.Mike grabbed Jayden back with force,his face slightly angered.J what the fuck is wrong with chu,you that thirsty for some dick,dick that been out here longer than you been in this fucking world dawg,dick that belongs to a nigga that used to feed ya ass bottles,and babysit ya ass? Mike questioned Jayden,his face serious,but confused at the same time.

And i fucking appreciate all that dawg,everything you did for me Mike,but im not going sit here and front like im not fucking attracted to you man,im just keeping it real,Jayden explained himself,his eyes still on Mike.Nigga you kissed me dawg,evidently ya ass aint that straight yourself,you wasn't like a father then nigga,Jayden spoke,waiting for Mike to respond.I aint going let this shit go down that road J,nigga i took care of you like you was my own man,and that's why this shit is crazy,i would be wrong as shit to mess with chu J,and im pissed off at myself too,i shouldn't had kissed you like that man,i mean,i always kissed you,but that shit felt different this time dawg,way fucking different,nigga i almost forgot who you was to me at that point,that shit made me feel like a weak ass nigga,letting a little dude i watched grow up get my dick hard,Mike explained to Jayden as Jayden listened carefully to his words.

Alright,i got chu Mike,we aint going take it down that road dawg,Jayden murmured silently,his face saddened.Nigga im not trying hurt ya feelings,im just not down with this man,and you shouldn't be either,Mike spoke softly to Jayden,seeing Jayden's saddened facial expression.Your soft ass,dont be like that nigga,Mike smirked at Jayden,giving Jayden a warm kiss on the forehead,wanting to see a smile on Jayden's face,instead of seeing the saddened facial expression he wore.Mike's lips moved from Jayden's forehead down to Jayden's cheek,and then to Jayden's lips again.This shit aint fucking right man,Mike exhaled with an annoyed facial expression on his face,slowly removing his lips from Jayden's,feeling the temptation to give into his lust for Jayden take over him again.

Dont fight that shit nigga,Jayden said silently to Mike,knowing that Mike was struggling with himself mentally and physically.Mike had never felt sexual desires for Jayden when Jayden was just a child,only love and protective instincts to keep Jayden safe,but now things were a little different,and now Mike had found himself slowly but surely becoming attracted to Jayden.A part of Mike still looked at Jayden as the little boy he used to watch years ago,but a part of him saw Jayden as a mature young man now,a young man he was now attracted to,not by choice,but by chance.Nigga what chu want with a nigga like me,im old school nigga,too old for you man,why you aint rolling with them younger brothas J? Mike said quietly,his eyes on Jayden's face.It aint got nothing to do with age dawg,aint no dude made me feel the way you do man,niggas can kill me for it,hate me for it,it is what it is,Jayden said calmly,his face blank.

Many dudes i woulda fucked up for saying some shit like that to me J,but chu my little dude,nigga you then did some shit to me man,for real tho man,Mike smiled thinly at Jayden.Mike was very attractive to Jayden,regardless of the previous relationship they had then and now.Mike was well kept,no matter how old he was.Mike grazed his cheek along Jayden's,his heart racing,and his breathing heavy.Mike then eased his lips towards Jayden's,letting them smoothly slide across Jayden's as he and Jayden moaned silently.Mike placed his arm around Jayden as he began to softly kiss him on the lips.Mike and Jayden's kiss became intense as they began to grope and feel each other.Yea nigga,You still going be Mike to me man,im still going be ya little homey,Jayden moaned out as he and Mike continued to kiss passionately.You want cha Mike in you nigga,huh baby boy? Mike whispered into Jayden's ear as they held each other.

Yea nigga,fuck yea,Jayden whispered back to Mike,their breathing becoming heavier and heavier.You want it on the couch or the bed nigga? Mike moaned silently to Jayden.Fuck all that,it dont matter dawg,Jayden moaned.Get on the couch man,Mike murmured to Jayden as Jayden eased himself on the sofa,laying himself down on the soft cushions.Mike studied Jayden's sculpted and slightly slender body with his eyes,his eyes examining every part of Jayden with desire.Jayden studied Mike's body also,lust in his thoughts.Mike hovered himself over Jayden,his face above Jayden's stare.You want me to get on my stomach man? Jayden questioned Mike softly and quietly as he and Mike stared at each other.Naw,stay on ya back baby,i wanna see ya face,Mike explained softly to Jayden.Jayden studied the growing bulge in Mike's towel as Mike grabbed a condom from his coat pocket.Mike tore open the condom with his teeth,and then unwrapped his towel from his waist,letting it fall underneath his tight flexing buttocks.Jayden could see Mike's well endowed penis in full view now as Mike eased the condom down slowly on it.

Mike pulled the towel from Jayden's waist and then positioned himself closer to Jayden,their naked bodies making close contact.Mike placed his chin above Jayden's forehead as he slid himself slowly and smoothly into Jayden.Jayden flinched just a little as Mike entered him.Mike's mouth widened as he began to thrust back and forth into Jayden as Jayden moaned silently.You like it little dude? Mike murmured softly to Jayden as he continued to enter Jayden gently and smoothly.Jayden pulled his arms around Mike,his fingers gripping Mike's smooth and strong back as he and Mike continued to have sexual intercourse.Mike gave

Jayden a soft kiss on the lips as they rocked back and forth in an intense friction.Mike enjoyed himself and so did Jayden.Mike pressed his face into Jayden's neck as he plunged in a rhythm,causing Jayden to moan out.

Shit man,damn! Jayden moaned,pushing Mike deeper into him.Jayden caressed the back of Mike's head as Mike kept stroking along,and then placed his fingers against Mike's face as Mike began to gently nibble on them.Mike began to pick up the pace,stroking himself inside of Jayden faster than before as Jayden began to masturbate himself.You want that hot cum on you baby boy? Mike moaned to Jayden,feeling himself about to orgasm.Hell yea nigga,Jayden moaned back.Mike thrusted himself into Jayden a few more times and then quickly pulled himself out of Jayden,ripping the condom from his penis,and then exploding his semen all over Jayden's bare abs as Jayden exploded with him.Three more rounds shot from Mike's erect penis as he moaned and grunted in pleasure,soaking Jayden in his semen.

Jayden moaned along with Mike in intense ecstasy,he and Mike both climaxing at nearly the same time.Mike dried Jayden off with the towel that laid under him,and then laid himself on top of Jayden,giving Jayden a soft kiss on the lips as they both inhaled and exhaled heavily.Jayden and Mike held each other throughout the rest of the night,until they both fell asleep.

Chapter 6

The sunlight dimly shined into the living area where Jayden and Mike slept,it was now morning.Jayden opened his eyes slowly,seeing Mike cuddled next to him on the sofa,his eyes shut.Jayden enjoyed feeling Mikes breath brush across his neck,just having Mike this close to him made him flutter inside.Jayden looked down at himself and then Mike,realizing that they had slept in the nude,side by side,after having sexual intercourse the previous night.Mike opened his eyes as his arm wrapped around Jayden tightly.You sleep good baby boy? Mike whispered to Jayden as Jayden stared him in the eyes.Fuck yea,you?

Jayden said silently to Mike.Hell to the yea,last night was off the chain nigga,Mike smiled thinly at Jayden as Jayden smiled back.

yea,it was dawg,Jayden smirked.Can i kiss you again man? Jayden questioned Mike softly.We laying up here ass naked nigga,you might as well nigga,Mike answered Jayden with a smile.Jayden gently pushed his lips towards Mike's as Mike pushed his towards Jayden's,their lips met softly.I love you J,i do man,Mike said silently to Jayden as their lips departed.Same here man,Jayden said silently back to Mike.Jayden and

Mike's eyes met as they gently pushed their foreheads together in an intimate stare.Man,J i been thinking man,fuck P,i dont want chu to live a life of crime man,by killing P ass,i shoulda never asked you some shit like that from the getgo,but i am going deal with that nigga man,i got to,Mike spoke silently to Jayden as Jayden listened clearly.Naw,forget P man,and Lenny,let's just wait for my moms to get better,and then we just leave this joint dawg,i got a little money on me,Jayden explained to Mike,no longer wanting Mike to take the lives of P or Lenny,not wanting Mike to end up in prison.

Fuck that J,P ass need to be six feet under little dude,im still thinking about all the shit he did to you man,that shit is unacceptable dude,Mike spoke to Jayden,his face serious.Let that shit fly man,it's you and me now dawg,you all i need man,not revenge dawg,Jayden explained softly to Mike.You a soft ass little nigga,that shit sexy in a way tho,Mike smiled softly at Jayden,his big hands gently latching onto Jayden's.Mike pulled himself on top of Jayden,he and Jayden's hands locked together.Give me kiss nigga,Mike said smoothly and silently to Jayden as he towered over him.Jayden eased his lips towards Mike's,giving Mike a warm kiss as Mike kissed him back with passion.Mike gave Jayden one more kiss and then headed into the bathroom,leaving Jayden on the sofa.Jayden sat silently on the sofa as Mike peeped his head from the bathroom door.Come on nigga,come get in the shower wit me! Mike spoke to Jayden as Jayden rose himself to his feet slowly,grabbing he and Mike's previously used towels from the sofa and floor,tossing them into the hamper,seeing Mike turn on the showerhead as he entered the bathroom.

Mike entered the bathtub first and then Jayden slowly stepped in afterwards.Mike swiftly reached for Jayden,pulling Jayden closely to him,hot water cascading down their wet naked bodies.Im going give you all the love you need baby boy,just let me nigga,i got chu J,you the missing piece to my puzzle little dude,i aint never loved no nigga or broad as much as i love you dawg,Mike whispered to Jayden as they held each other tightly,the showerhead raining down on them.I love you too man,i really do tho dawg,man i then forgot about my dude Delonte man,man that's how much you got me hooked Mike,Jayden explained to Mike as they continued to embrace.Jayden and Mike were both in love and in lust,but most of all,in love.

What the fuck,you hear that J? Mike whispered,hearing a slight sound catch his ears.The bathroom door slowly flew open just as Jayden was about to speak.Jayden and Mike was now staring Tracey in the eyes as she stood speechless at the bathroom door,her face blank as she witnessed both Jayden and Mike standing naked under the running showerhead,tightly embracing each other like lovers,and they were.I dont believe this bullshit,in my own motherfucking house,i should have saw this shit,Tracey said silently and very calmly,her eyes on Mike and Jayden.Tracey gave Mike and Jayden one more glance,and then shook her head in disappointment,and then quietly leaving out the bathroom afterwards.Ma wait man! Jayden spoke out,quickly exiting the bathtub,his body naked and soaking wet.Tracey! Mike spoke,stepping out of the bathtub also,quickly shrugging into his clothes as Jayden did the same.Jayden and Mike quickly exited the bathroom,fully dressed again,both of them following behind Tracey,wanting to explain themselves to her.

Ma wait! Jayden spoke again,gently grabbing Tracey by her arm before she could move any further.Jayden i watched you get raped by some nasty motherfucking men,then i come home and see this bullshit,i had a miscarriage,was raped my damn self,i cant take no more,Tracey explained to Jayden,hurt in her face.I know ma,i know man,Jayden tried to comfort Tracey as tears began to slowly slide down her face.And Mike,dont chu say a motherfucking word to me! Tracey yelled out,seeing Mike about to speak.Tracey's face became nearly deranged as she grabbed Jayden tightly by his arm.How long this shit being going on Jayden,he been messing with chu since you was little,you better tell me the motherfucking truth?! Tracey questioned Jayden,her eyes examining Jayden and then Mike,and then back to Jayden.Naw ma,that dude never once touched me like that man,P was the one doing fucked up shit to me man,not Mike,Jayden explained to Tracey,slightly afraid of her,even tho he was an adult now,seeing her raw authority side come out brought out the child in him again,even bringing tears to his eyes.

Tracey calm down man,let me fucking explain alright,Mike said calmly.Mike i know you betta shut the fuck up talking to me,i am not in the mood right motherfucking now,My motherfucking son tho Mike?! Tracey shouted,her nose spread.Tracey i love that boy,i never did no nasty shit to him when he was little,you know that shit,that nigga was my heart man,and you sitting here trying say i molested the little dude,i aint hearing that man,man,Jayden just got me feeling all kinds of shit about him now,shit i cant motherfucking control,but i never once touched J when he was little,i should be popped had i did man,i love that fucking boy,now i love him,and im in love with him Tracey! Mike explained to Tracey,his face serious.Even if you didn't motherfucking touch J when he was little Mike i still cannot believe im hearing this motherfucking shit? Tracey said,stress,anger and confusion in her face,Jayden and Mike's sudden romance just added more turmoil to the turmoil she and Jayden had already experienced with P and the others.

Tracey had released herself from the hospital early,after recovering a bit,and now was shocked,confused and deeply disappointed at the events she was living through at this moment,her witnessing Mike,a man who helped her with Jayden as a child and adult Jayden himself in an intimate position,a position she wasn't too fond of,a position that also raised questions for her,was Mike having sexually intimate encounters with Jayden when he was a child,tho Mike had not,only looking at Jayden as a child then,having only love and affection for him,Tracey somewhat thought otherwise.

Mike what about that shit chu pulled awhile back,when Jarrelle told me you had answered the door naked wit Jayden? I mean,i didn't think nothing of it,you could've left Jayden by hisself,so i respect that chu took him wit chu,but now that shit is making sense to me? Tracey spoke,her eyes on Mike as Mike stared back.Nothing fucking happened man,you know aint nothing happen,you just trying to take the shit P then did out on me man,i aint stupid,Mike explained to Tracey.Mike you dont understand,you not a parent,this shit is killing me Mike,this shit going put me in my grave early if p and em aint,Tracey explained to Mike,her face strained and tired.I feel you man,i feel you Tracey,Mike said softly.

J are you sure he never touched you? Tracey asked Jayden again,her eyes on Jayden's face.Im sure ma,sit down tho man,why you leave the hospital? Jayden said softly to Tracey,easing her onto one of the dining room chairs.Tracey placed her face into her palm,and then sighed silently as Jayden and Mike watched her in silence,and then staring over at each other.Life is full of fucking surprises,Jayden i asked you many times over was you gay,and you said no,right or wrong? Tracey spoke to Jayden,her eyes locking on him.You right ma,but yea,i am man,Jayden finally admitted to Tracey,honesty in his face.Come here baby,Tracey spoke silently to Jayden as Jayden approached her.Tracey placed her arm around Jayden,and then began to speak.Jayden you still my child,i dont agree wit this,men should be with women,but chu still my child and i love you okay,Tracey said to Jayden,two tears rolling down her face.I love you too ma,Jayden spoke,tears now rolling from his face as he and Tracey hugged.

Open up the door man! Jarrelle yelled as he banged violently against the front door,causing every head in the apartment to turn towards the sound.I got it man,Mike spoke silently as he headed towards the front door,opening the front door slightly,seeing Jarrelle's face through the crack.Let me in nigga,we need to converse,man to man dawg! Jarrelle said to Mike.Nigga i aint scared of you,it aint nothing dawg,Mike spoke as he flung the door open,letting Jarrelle enter.Nigga i thought about some shit,you been fucking wit my son for a minute nigga,that's why he gay,aint it?! Jarrelle said to Mike as he bounced up and down on his tiptoes,his fists balled up,wanting to combat Mike.Nigga you tripping dawg,but i got something for ya ass dawg,Mike said calmly as he placed up his own fists,preparing himself to fight Jarrelle.

Nigga we can duke it out dawg! Jarrelle shouted as he and Mike began to swing at each other.Come on man,ya'll tripping man,not now ya'll! Jayden spoke to Jarrelle and Mike,not wanting them to fight.Nigga you some shit,Mike blurted out as Jarrelle gave him a swift punch to the jaw.Naw,you the weak ass nigga dawg,Jarrelle said to Mike as he swung at Mike again.Mike avoided two more of Jarrelle's shots,and then gave Jarrelle a right hand jab and then a left hand jab,causing Jarrelle to stumble slightly,but not fall.Take that shit out the house ya'll! Tracey yelled at Jarrelle and Mike as they continued to swing at each other.Mike then charged at Jarrelle,knocking him to the hardwood floor,and then placing Jarrelle's arms behind his back,restraining him.Yea nigga,what now?! Mike shouted at Jarrelle as Jarrelle struggled to break free of Mike's strong grip.Nigga do you give a shit about ya son? Mike yelled at Jarrelle.Get the fuck off me nigga! Jarrelle yelled at Mike.

Nigga i know them niggas fucked wit cha head,raping ya fucking son right in front of you,that shit hurt dont it,nigga you aint that tough,that shit got chu heated nigga,no man wanna see or hear about some shit like that happening to their son,you wanna kill them niggas,you already dealt wit one of em,i know how you feel man,i love J too,Mike spoke,tears rolling down his face as he still kept Jarrelle locked in his grip.I know you in pain nigga,tell ya son that shit,tell J that,Mike said softly as he released Jarrelle from his grip,allowing Jarrelle to stand to his feet again.You aint nothing but a pussy ass nigga! Jarrelle swung at Mike,his voice cracking and his eyes watery,Mike's words were getting to him.I aint even going fight chu no more dawg,Mike said silently,allowing Jarrelle to yank him up by the collar,seeing the tears in Jarrelle's eyes,feeling some sympathy for him.Talk to ya fucking son,tell him you care for him nigga,life is short motherfucker,niggas dying day by day,hug the little dude,be a father,that's ya little shawty dude,i love him just as much as you do,let him know that not all men are like P and em other motherfuckers,let him know how a real man is,i did,now it's your turn my man,Mike explained to Jarrelle as Jarrelle released his collar.

Come over here for a second Jayden,Jarrelle choked out as Jayden slowly headed towards him.Yea pops? Jayden said silently,his face confused and scared.Jarrelle gave Jayden a blank tearful stare and then tightly and swiftly wrapped his arms around Jayden in an embrace as he broke out into even more tears,shocking Jayden,and even Tracey.

Jarrelle held Jayden in his arms for nearly ten minutes.I love you

Jayden,you know that,i know i wasn't around all the time,but imma be around now alright,true shit,Jarrelle whispered in Jayden's ear as he continued to embrace Jayden.Tracey and Mike watched Jayden and Jarrelle from the sidelines,both of them silent and still.Jayden being same sex oriented and also being romantically involved with Mike wasn't the only thing that troubled Jarrelle,Jayden being sexually humiliated in front of him was the thing that caused him the most trouble.Jarrelle wanted to reestablish his role as Jayden's father,wanting to be more a part of Jayden's life this time around,seeing Jayden humiliated opened his eyes,it made him realize just how easily Jayden could be tooken advantage of,and how lonely and helpless Jayden could be without him or Mike,especially in a world where some were just as vile as P and the others.

Chapter 7

Jayden and Jarrelle developed more of a relationship over the weeks that passed,Jarrelle wanting to be more of a father to Jayden,Jarrelle and Tracey even began to mend things between them as well,Jarrelle flirting with Tracey every now and then.Tho Tracey and Jarrelle got used to Jayden and Mike developing a romantic interest with each other they still had trouble fully accepting it,but knowing that Mike deeply loved and cared for their son Jayden made things a little easier.Jayden and Mike sat side by side on the sofa as they lip locked,but quickly stopped once Jarrelle entered the living area,knowing Jarrelle wasn't quite ready to see them show affection so openly,wanting to show him just a bit of respect.Thank you,i dont wanna see that mess,ya'll think i aint see that shit,please,Jarrelle frowned at Mike and Jayden as he sat at the dining room table.Tsk,I dont see how you allow another nigga,another man,treat you like his bitch,his woman,shit got me clueless? Jarrelle spoke to Jayden,his eyes on the tv screen.

Not today pops,Jayden smirked slightly.Alright,but im just saying Jayden,Jarrelle said,now sipping a cup of orange juice.Jayden not my bitch

Jarrelle,he my little dude,my partner dawg,Mike said calmly to Jarrelle as Jarrelle listened.Whatever man,ya'll do ya'll thang,if you like young boy booty that's on you,but that's my son you fucking,my flesh and blood,so in a way you violating me too my homey,remember that,Jarrelle said to Mike,his eyes on Mike's face.Man it's sunday,i aint no christian,but ya ass aint going take me outta my zone today Jarrelle,i aint going let chu dawg,Mike chuckled softly.Yea right nigga,you told Jayden you waisted motherfuckers before Mike,Jayden aint wit that,he the soft type,i did my research nigga,big Mike,that's what they call em,you know about that Jayden? Jarrelle spoke,his eyes scanning both Mike and Jayden's faces.

I already know about Mike past dad,the dude pratically raised me,when you wasn't even there,Jayden blurted out silently.Did you hear what chu said sonny boy,you said raised? Jarrelle said to Jayden as Jayden shook his head in response,wanting Jarrelle to stop with the nagging.If you said raised,that mean in some ways that nigga like a father to you,you wanna piece of me too Jayden,you want pops to smash you too,because that's what chu saying homeboy,that shit is nasty man,Jarrelle said to Jayden,disappointment behind his eyes.Im done pops,let's go in my room Mike,Jayden said as he rose from the sofa,Mike following behind him.You was wrong as shit for that Jarrelle,you taken it too far man,Mike spoke before entering Jayden's room.Come on man,leave it alone,Jayden said silently to Mike,softly pulling Mike into the room with him,shutting the door behind them.Tracey! Ay Tracey!

Jarrelle called out to Tracey.What Jarrelle?! Tracey said,her face annoyed.You letting that nigga stay up in here wit our son like that? Jarrelle asked Tracey,his eyes on her face.Mike alright,he been around Jayden all his life,he cool,i dont let him spend the night over here,so everything cool,and to keep it real,i never seen Jayden so damn happy before Mike came back into his life,leave them alone Jarrelle,come in my room,i got something to show you,Tracey spoke to Jarrelle.

You got something to show me huh? Jarrelle said,a smirk on his face.Yea,i sure damn do nigga,come on,Tracey said smoothly and seductively,grabbing Jarrelle by his arm,pulling him out of the dining room chair.Jarrelle allowed Tracey to pull him into her bedroom,the bedroom door shutting softly as they entered.It was soon midnight,and the house was quiet and dark,only dimly lit by a few lights.Mike usually went home around this time,but he and Jayden had fell asleep together,and Tracey didn't bother to say anything.Mike shook Jayden's arm gently,wanting Jayden to wake up.Jayden opened his eyes quickly,feeling Mike tugging against his arm.Hey man,Jayden yarned,giving Mike a gentle kiss on the lips as he sat up.Everybody sleep,let's get in the shower,i think Jarrelle ass gone,Mike whispered to Jayden,seduction in his eyes.Naw man,my moms probably still woke dawg,Jayden whispered back to Mike.Naw,i think she sleep,aint nobody in the living room,come on dawg,i can bang that shit in the shower baby boy,you know you like that freaky shit nigga,Mike smiled at Jayden.

Jayden became silent for awhile,but then began to speak again.Alright man,we gotta keep it on the low tho man,i dont want my mother to hear us,Jayden whispered to Mike as he and Mike stood to their feet.Jayden and Mike tiptoed into the bathroom near Jayden's room,and then began shrugging out of all of their clothes once they entered,shutting and locking the bathroom door afterwards.Take that shit off little nigga,let me see that body dawg,Mike licked his lips as Jayden took off his last piece of clothing,now standing fully naked in front of Mike as Mike stood fully naked in front of him.Jayden and Mike then stepped into the bathtub,Jayden turning on the showerhead as they entered.Mike grabbed Jayden by his waist,stilling a gentle and quick kiss from Jayden's lips as the water ran down on them.Mike dont get mad dawg,but i cant handle you leaving me for somebody else dawg,you might find a broad or another dude and roll out on my ass,but nigga i could deal wit chu having side pieces,just dont fucking leave me dawg,jayden spoke to Mike as Mike stared back at him with a confused facial expression.

Leave you,nigga i been wit chu since day one dawg,i aint going nowhere little homey,like i said,you my little dude nigga,give me a hug nigga,you my little dude for life,Mike said softly to Jayden,yanking Jayden in his arms,holding him tightly.Mike began to kiss Jayden on the forehead as they continued to embrace,Jayden could now feel Mike's erection on his thigh.My bad dawg,the shit chu do to me nigga,Mike smiled thinly at Jayden,knowing Jayden had realized that he had a hard on.Jayden kneeled to his knees,wanting to give Mike's erection a taste.Oh shit! Mike blurted out,feeling Jayden's cheek and lips brush across his erection.Naw man,you going get my ass a ticket into hell little nigga,fucking you was one thing,now you about to give me head J,i aint violating you like that man,Mike explained,quickly pulling Jayden to his feet.We can fuck,but i aint going put my thing in ya mouth,that's wrong J,you my baby boy nigga,i aint doing that,Mike further explained to Jayden,grabbing Jayden into his arms again,kissing him softly on the lips as Jayden returned the favor.

Jayden and Mike stayed in the shower for another hour,and then finally exited the steam filled bathroom,pulling short white towels around their waists while stepping their feet into shower shoes.Jayden and Mike's eyes widened as they saw Jarrelle exiting from the other bathroom near Tracey's bedroom,soaking wet,wearing nothing but a towel around his waist,just as they were.Imma act like i aint see shit,a nigga just wanted to take a shower,wash his ass,and he come out to see his son and his son man taking a shower of their own,im getting too old for this shit,Jarrelle spoke,his eyes on Jayden and Mike.

Jayden and Mike headed towards Jayden's bedroom,wanting to avoid a confrontation with Jarrelle.Ya'll niggas aint got to be scared,ya'll trying watch some flicks wit a nigga? Jarrelle smirked at Jayden and Mike.What kind of flicks? Jayden questioned Jarrelle.A flick nigga,you about to be 19 soon and you dont know what a porno flick is? Jarrelle smiled thinly at Jayden.I guess Mike aint teach you as much as i thought?

Jarrelle chuckled softly.Oh,yea,i know what porn is dawg,i aint that stupid pop,you just caught me off guard,Jayden smiled.Pop the shit in,Mike said to Jarrelle with ease.Jarrelle headed over to the tv and then pulled a dvd from out of his bag that rested under the coffe table,placing it into the dvd player as Jayden and Mike sat side by side on the sofa.Jarrelle joined them on the sofa,sitting next to Jayden,and then pushing the play button on the remote controller,starting the adult flick.Loud moans and noises erupted from the tv as Jarrelle Jayden and

Mike sat silently on the sofa in nothing but their towels,watching some young woman bounce up and down on a young mans private part,moans escaping her lips.

The chick is phat as shit,but her grill need a little work tho,Jarrelle said to Jayden and Mike.True,Mike said,his eyes still on the tv screen.Dude giving it to her,he can stroke,Jayden complimented the man on the tv screen as Mike turned his gaze towards him.Is that right nigga? Mike said to Jayden,a smirk on his face,he was kind of Jealous of Jayden's comment towards the male adult star on the tv set.Shid,you was talking about that chick dude,Jayden smiled at Mike as Mike softly reached for his hand,making sure Jarrelle couldn't see him do it.Tho Mike and Jarrelle had their differences,they all bonded over the adult flick that played on the tv screen,in some ways their bonding technique was akward,but it sufficed.Their rods stood at the tv screen just as much as their eyes,this lasted for an hour,until they all wanted the real thing.Let's freak nigga,Mike whispered into Jayden's ear as Tracey entered the living area,seeing the three on the sofa,her eyes widening as she examined the tv screen.

That is so damn nasty,ya'll some nasty motherfuckers,all ya'll,Tracey sighed,but in somes ways she was happy,seeing that they got along just fine at that moment.Tracey gave Jayden a kiss on the forehead and then placed her arm around Jarrelle's neck,her cleavage showing just a bit through her silk gown.Tsk,ma,im sitting right here man,Jayden smiled slightly.Nigga this dick made you,Jarrelle smirked at Jayden as he rose from the sofa.Im sorry baby,we about to leave ya'll alone tho,Tracey spoke to Jayden as she pulled Jarrelle towards her bedroom.Hold on for a second Trace,Jarrelle said to Tracey,using her nickname.Jarrelle reached into his bag and then pulled a latex condom from it,and then softly placing it into Jayden's hand,giving Jayden a little dap afterwards.Keep that shit safe wit my son Mike,jarrelle said to Mike,his face serious.I got chu dawg,he in good hands man,peace out,Mike said to Jarrelle as he and Jayden watched Him and Tracey go into the bedroom,closing the door behind them afterwards.

Come on baby boy,let's hit them sheets,Mike whispered to Jayden as he and Jayden headed into Jayden's bedroom,closing the door behind them.Mike stood next to Jayden as they watched each other intensely with lust.Mike gave Jayden a soft kiss on the lips,and then began to kiss Jayden all over his body,kissing Jayden's pecks,navel,abs,and even his thighs,as Jayden moaned softly,enjoying himself.My turn nigga,Jayden spoke as he kneeled to his knees,reaching his hand underneath Mike's towel,placing the tip of Mike's penis into his mouth,licking the tip first,and then easing his tongue around the shaft as Mike moaned out just a little.Jayden then swallowed Mike's penis into his mouth,letting it reach his throat as he gagged back and forth on it in a fast friction,a friction that caused Mike to quiver and moan,and then bite down on his lip in pleasure as he felt himself precum just a little in Jayden's mouth.Go ahead J,you about to make me bust nigga! Mike moaned deeply,quickly pulling himself from jayden's mouth before he could erupt his semen into jayden's mouth.

Mike placed Jayden on the bed,spreading Jayden's legs,placing one of Jayden's legs above his waist as he pushed himself into Jayden with gentle force.You going take this dick on this bed nigga,Mike moaned to Jayden as Jayden moaned silently,his head resting on his pillow.Jayden could feel Mike slide deeper inside him as Mike pushed his crotch closer to him,their pubic hairs brushing against each other as Mike began to thrust and pound Jayden,both of them moaning in pleasure.Ah,shit nigga! Jayden dragged the words out slowly as Mike continued to make love to him.Jayden could hear Tracey and Jarrelle wrecking the headboards of Tracey's bed as he and Mike did their own thing,but he paid it no attention,he was glad to see his mother with someone other than P,and he was also busy himself at the moment.Mike raised himself higher above Jayden,slamming and massaging himself deeper into Jayden as Jayden stroked himself from under his towel,getting a great amount of pleasure from it.Mike then pressed his face into Jayden's cheek,stroking even harder as Jayden moaned louder,unable to control himself.Give me that shit,open that ass up nigga,Mike whispered to Jayden as he stroked back and forth into Jayden,Jayden pulling his arms around Mike's sweaty back,his fingers slightly slipping off of Mike's moist flesh.

Mike pulled his towel from his waist,letting it drop to the bedroom floor as he continued to penetrate into Jayden.Take this shit off,Mike moaned to Jayden,yanking Jayden's towel from his waist as well,wanting to see all of Jayden's nakedness,and wanting Jayden to see his nakedness as well.Mike's posterior flexed and bounced slightly as he dug into Jayden,Jayden's thighs around his waist.You want me to take that stuff nigga,give me that ass little dude,that shit mine nigga! Mike moaned and grunted to Jayden,biting down on his lip,his eyes staring directly into Jayden's as his nude body continued to thrust into Jayden's nude body.Jayden placed his hand around Mike's head as his own head hit against the headboard,making tapping sounds just as loud as Mike's slapping Genitals that hit against Jayden.Mike leaned his face down towards Jayden,as Jayden's mouth flew open in intense pleasure and thrill.You want something in that mouth nigga? Mike moaned silently to Jayden,seeing Jayden's mouth wide open.Yea nigga,yea! Jayden moaned back to Mike,holding tightly to Mike's strong muscular arms with one hand,while the other stroked himself.

Mike tucked his tonuge into Jayden's mouth,giving Jayden's smooth lips a good taste.Jayden and Mike kept at it for hours,Mike even thrusting Jayden from the side angle,his huge penis working into Jayden's body even as they resumed their previous position.Damn nigga,we aint use a condom dawg,Mike moaned,realizing he was entering into Jayden without anything,just bare flesh against bare flesh.Imma stop baby boy,Mike said,knowing he could erupt at any moment now.Fuck naw man,bust off in me nigga,Jayden said silently to Mike as Mike continued to thrust.You want that cum nigga,you want that cum up in you nigga,imma give it to you nigga! Mike moaned out,feeling himself about to release.Jayden shot out before Mike could,soaking his abs with his own semen as Mike orgasmed,loading Jayden up with his hot and thick semen,both of them moaning and hissing in deep pleasure and complete ecstasy,ending their love making session with a intense and passion filled kiss.

Mike fell onto Jayden,not removing himself from Jayden,but laid his naked sweaty body against Jayden's naked sweaty body as they both breathed and quivered heavily,holding each other to sleep,the scent of manly sweat and musk scenting the room.

Chapter 8

Jayden and Mike slept the night away,until the sun shined outside,beating against their naked bodies.Jayden stood to his feet,and then gave Mike a kiss on the lips before leaving out his bedroom,wanting to clean himself up a bit,sticky and musky from his intense and romantic night with Mike.Jayden quickly hopped into the shower,but could hear someone enter the bathroom with him as he stepped into the bathtub,it was Mike.You left me in the room nigga,Mike joked,his eyes on Jayden.Jayden chuckled in response to Mike's words as Mike joined him in the shower,both of them washing away the steamy sex from the other night,shrugging themselves into clean clothes after they were done.The apartment was empty,only Jayden and Mike were there,there was no sign of Tracey or Jarrelle.

Jayden even checked Tracey's bedroom,still there was no sign of her or Jarrelle.Jayden and Mike used their alone time to snuggle on the sofa side by side,and then began playing video games a little later after that.Man i got something to ask you J? Mike spoke to Jayden,his eyes still on the tv screen,and his hands still on his controller.Go ahead nigga,say what chu gotta say,Jayden spoke to Mike,still pushing and pulling on his controller.On the real,i want chu to move in wit me J,would you be cool wit that man? Mike questioned Jayden softly,placing his controller down,his eyes studying Jayden's face.You serious dawg? Jayden said to Mike,his face shocked.Hell yea im serious,we been doing this for awhile now,now i think it's time for you to come stay at my crib nigga,my place would be ya place nigga,you can walk around butt ass naked if you want,Mike explained to Jayden as Jayden listened carefully.

Damn nigga,you catching me off guard today,Jayden smiled.Stop trying change the subject nigga,you trying move in or what? Mike smiled thinly at Jayden,still waiting on Jayden to give him an answer.Jayden pondered to himself for just a few seconds and then gave Mike an answer.Yea nigga,i move in wit chu,Jayden said softly to Mike,his eyes on Mike's smirking face.Cool,that's what's up,start packing ya shit then nigga,Mike spoke to Jayden,a grin on his face.Mike wanted to take he and Jayden's relationship to a new level,wanting Jayden to come live with him,and not caring who thought anything bad of it.You want me to pack now nigga? Jayden spoke,his face confused.Yea nigga,let's roll out this joint today,Mike smiled at Jayden as Jayden stood to his feet.Alright,imma about to go pack and shit,Jayden said to Mike before heading into his bedroom.Jayden packed all of his things and rolled his suitcase out his bedroom,giving his nearly empty bedroom one more glance before shutting his bedroom door.

Let's roll baby boy,Mike murmured to Jayden as they headed towards the front door,Jayden holding one of his suitcases while Mike held onto the other,his free arm around Jayden.Tracey and Jarrelle entered the apartment as Jayden and Mike were about to leave,their eyes all making contact.Where ya'll going? Tracey questioned Jayden and Mike,seeing them packed and ready to leave out the front door.Im moving in wit Mike ma,Jayden said timidly and softly.What,naw,it's cool,you can stay here as long as you want baby,you aint gotta move out,im cool wit chu and Mike,you used to put up wit P and his mess,stay J,Tracey spoke to Jayden,her face sort of saddened and worried.Jayden now im cool wit chu and this nigga doing ya'll thang now,but chu still a young buck,give it time,stay wit cha moms for a little while longer boy,even tho i wasn't much of a father,this one thing i hope you listen to man,Jarrelle explained to Jayden.Im cool,Jayden spoke to Tracey and Jarrelle,a happy smile on his face.Alright baby,whatever you say wit cha grown ass,Tracey smiled softly at Jayden,thinking about the journey she and Jayden had been through,through all the years.

Tracey wasn't the best mother,but she did love Jayden,and really didn't want to see him leave,especially so soon.Tracey grabbed Jayden into her arms,holding onto him tightly,tears wanting to form in her eyes as she began to whisper to him.You know this is always your home,you can always come back baby,Tracey whispered to Jayden,and then finally letting him go.See you Tracey,i see ya ass around too Jarrelle,Mike murmured,giving Jarrelle dap,and then holding the front door open for Jayden.I see you around little man,Jarrelle said to Jayden,giving Jayden dap,but then swiftly giving him a huge and somewhat long hug.Bye pops,bye ma,Jayden spoke,keeping his tears back as he headed towards the front door with Mike.

Break this shit up! P shouted as he headed towards the front door,pushing Jayden and Mike back into the apartment,a gun in his hand,and Lenny behind him,a gun in his hand also.Mike reached for his gun in his coat pocket but P saw him,pointing his gun directly at Mike before Mike could fully grip his gun.Put cha motherfucking hands up nigga! P yelled at Mike as Mike placed his hands to the air.Chill the fuck out nigga! Mike yelled at P as Lenny closed the front door behind them,locking everyone inside the apartment.One of ya'll niggas popped my man Trey,that shit make me look weak my niggas,now i gotta smoke one of ya'll! P yelled at the group.Come here little nigga,P spoke to Jayden,as Jayden watched in fear.P leave J alone man! Mike yelled.Just leave me be man,leave me alone P,Jayden murmured,not wanting to move any closer to P.Imma shoot cha hoe ass bitch of mother in her fucking head if you dont come here little nigga! P yelled at Jayden.P leave him alone! Tracey yelled at P,scared of what P might do to Jayden.

Jayden moved closer to P,obeying P's words.P slapped Jayden with his gun once Jayden got closer,pistol whipping Jayden with it,causing Jayden to fall to the hardwood floor.That's enough nigga!! Mike shouted,fury in his voice,his hands about to grip his gun,but now he had Lenny's gun pointed at his head before he could do anything.P you fucking tripping nigga,kill me man,i popped Trey's pussy ass,now kill me motherfucker! Jarrelle shouted.So you getting buck wit it nigga,alright,P said calmly,pulling his gun towards Jarrelle,but became distracted by the taps against the front door of the apartment.Keep them niggas in line,P said to Lenny,kicking Jayden in his chest before going over to the front door.Who the fuck is it?! P spoke.It's Delonte,Jayden in there? Delonte spoke,having no clue that it was pure chaos going on inside the apartment.Yea,he is,P spoke,quickly opening the front door,and then yanking Delonte inside,pushing him to the floor beside Jayden.I didn't do shit man! Delonte explained,his hands in the air,seeing the gun in P's hand.I didn't say you did shit,shut the fuck up nigga! P yelled at Delonte.

Ya'll betta watch this shit! P spoke as he pulled Jayden to his feet.P yanked Jayden by his collar,and then began to repeatly punch jayden in the face,as everyone watched in anger and fear,Lenny smiling and chuckling at it.Jayden grunted out in pain,feeling the sting of P's punches.Mike was about to rush over to Jayden's aid,but was hit in the face by Lenny's gun,causing him to stumble backwards.Stop!! Tracey yelled at the top of her lungs,wanting P to stop hurting Jayden.Nigga you a pussy! Delonte shouted at P.P shoved Jayden to the floor and then began to beat Delonte instead,kicking Delonte in his chest,and then punching Delonte repeatly in the face,even harder than he hit Jayden.Blood soon started to leak from Delonte's nose and mouth as P continued to pummel him with force.

Little faggot ass nigga! P shouted at Delonte as he punched and punched Delonte,causing Delonte to block his face from his punches,tho P still continued to hit him.P finally let up on Delonte,and then turned his attention back to Jayden.Come here nigga,i aint done wit cha ass! P spoke to Jayden,snatching Jayden up by his collar,spitting in jayden's face,and then giving Jayden two punches to the stomach as Jayden gasped in pain.Lenny snickered as he watched P violently assualt Jayden again and again,but was soon charged by Jarrelle,too distracted to see Jarrelle coming his way.Lenny fell to the floor after being thrashed by Jarrelle,he and Jarrelle struggling,Lenny accidently dropping the gun from his hands.P quickly dropped Jayden from his grip,wanting to quickly make a run for the front door,seeing that Mike was about to reach into his coat pocket for his gun,and seeing that Lenny was no longer able to back him now.

P quickly headed for the front door,but was shot in his right leg,the gunshot wound causing him to stumble to the hardwood floor before he could make it to the door,his gun falling out of his hand,hitting the hardwood floor just as hard as he did.Ah Shit! P yelled out in pain,still trying to crawl towards the front door,hoping to escape.P felt another bullet pierce into his left leg as he screamed out in even more pain.P rolled to his side,seeing who it was who had shot him multiple times.P was now staring Tracey in the eyes as she stared back at him with deep rage in her eyes,bitterness and anger covering her flushed face,and Lenny's smoking gun in her hands,something she picked up while Jarrelle and Lenny were wrestling around on the floor.

Tracey wanted to give Jarrelle the same pain he caused Jayden,and her,but with a gun instead.Tracey,what the fuck is you doing girl?! P shouted out in pain,holding tightly to his legs,feeling the burning sting of the bullet wounds.Girl we had good times together man! P yelled out,still feeling intense pain.Tracey shot at P again,missing him accidently,not caring what P had to say to her at this point.Tracey fired the gun again,missing P again,her nerves rushing through her body and her hands trembling too rapidly to control the gun.Give me the gun Tracey,it's cool,Mike spoke softly,removing the gun from Tracey's hand,seeing that she was unfit to handle it at this point.What now nigga,imma faggot right nigga?!! Delonte yelled at P as he stood over him,P's gun in his hands,his voice cracking and blood still running from his nose.Delonte fuck that nigga,he aint worth going to jail for man! Jayden spoke.Naw,fuck that man,look what that dude did to me man,and all the shit he did to you dude! Delonte screamed,anger and rage in his face and voice,his eyes watery.

Delonte had no sympathy for P at this moment,only malice,and a need to end P's life.Nigga ya'll aint about that life,ya'll gay ass niggas,you know ya ass going be on lockdown if you kill me right nigga,and i got other niggas that's going pop ya ass for this shit dawg,dont be stupid nigga! P said to Delonte,hoping to scare Delonte out of doing something life threatening to him,not knowing that Delonte paid his words no attention.Delonte cocked the gun as he and P made eye contact.Tell ya homeboy to chill Jayden! P grunted,his eyes now on Jayden.Jayden could see the hidden fear in P's eyes as he and P made eye contact.Jayden gave P one more blank glance,and then shook his head in pity,turning his head away from P,not wanting to see what was about to happen next,not sure if he could stomach it.Dawg! P yelled at Delonte.

Delonte ignored P's last word and then pulled the trigger of the gun,shooting P in his chest as P yelled out in deep pain,now squirming on the floor in agony as blood rushed from his bullet wound to the chest,soaking his clothes.Delonte shot P three more times after that,ending P's life.Tho Jayden could not see P's death,he could still hear Delonte firing bullets into P's lifeless body.Jayden turned his head towards Jarrelle and Lenny,seeing Jarrelle stomp Lenny over and over again as Lenny laid bloodied and beaten on the floor,trying to block the blows from Jarrell's shoes.Delonte let the smoking gun fall from his shaking hands as he sat down on the floor next to P's dead body,his nostrils flaring,his own blood still staining his lips,nose,and his shirt.Everyone could now hear the police sirens going off outside of the apartment building.

Mike quickly headed over to Jayden,snatching Jayden into his arms,his chin above Jayden's forehead,his arms tightly around Jayden's body in an embrace.Tracey slowly headed over to Jayden as well,latching her arms around him from behind,tears streaming down her face.Jarrelle had finally eased up on Lenny,wanting the police to deal with him now,but then headed over to Jayden as well,pulling his arms around Jayden,joining the silent group hug.The entire apartment was silent.

Chapter 9

Jayden,Mike and the others told the police would had transpired in the apartment as the dead P was taken out of the apartment in a body bag,they recieved further questioning,but none of them were charged,with the exception of Lenny,tho the police wanted to charge Jarrelle with the death of

Trey,they had no hard evidence that he commited it.Lenny was sentenced to twenty one years in prison for involvement in attempted murder,no one ever saw him since.Delonte and Jayden continued their relationship,but only as friends,good friends,only one person had Jayden's heart,and that person was Mike.

Jayden had moved in with Mike,his name even being put on the lease.Tracey and Jarrelle had gotten married,something that shocked many,Tracey no longer bed hopped with random men,she had finally tied the knot with someone,someone

who was actually the father of her
son,Jayden.

Chapter 10

A year had passed,and Jayden and
Mike's relationship had grown even
further.Jayden was now 19 years
old,and now living with Mike,their
romance blissful and full of
excitement,rarely having any dull
moments.jayden and Mike sat on the
suade couch side by side,playing
video games together,their eyes

locked on the tv screen.You some shit in this game nigga,Mike smirked at Jayden.Naw,you some shit nigga,Jayden smirked back at Mike,a wide smile on his face.Mike placed his controller to the side,and then pulled Jayden closer to him.All jokes aside,i love you nigga,always man,you my little dude,my baby boy nigga,my heart man,my partner nigga,Mike spoke to Jayden with conviction.I love you too man,you my big Mike,Jayden smiled at Mike,but then his face turning serious.Man i never thought i would be telling another dude this shit,but this shit shows you that love aint got no color or no gender man,but i truly do have mad love for you J,mad motherfucking love baby,Mike spoke,his eyes glassy,his face sincere.Jayden smiled thinly in response,a shy smile.

Mike held onto Jayden tighter as he and Jayden made direct eye contact.Tho Mike was attracted to women,he had discovered that he could give another male the same love and affection he would a woman,tho he feared it at first he eventually embraced it.Jayden and Mike loved each other both physically and emotionally.And tho Mike loved Jayden since he was a child,he had grown to love the adult Jayden in more ways than one,loving Jayden,and being in love with Jayden,something he thought was taboo,but learned to accept.Both jayden and Mike had small tears slowly and smoothly running down their faces as they began to kiss passionately,Jayden slowly and softly dropping his controller behind him as he and Mike continued to kiss,the song live your life by the rapper Ti playing in the background,echoing from outside of Jayden and Mike's home.Jayden and Mike kissed again the day after that,and the day after that.

The end.

Note from the author of His uncles or His daddies?

For those who are confused or want to know,Mike isn't a pedophile,if he was,trust me,i would have stated that in the story,i wasn't shy about creating a rape scene or a scene where someone gets unrinated on,then i would not be shy to state that Mike's intentions were to sexually abuse Jayden years ago,not adult Jayden,but baby Jayden.Mike had love for Jayden when he was a child,and still does,not sexual attraction,but on many occasions people can sometimes develope many other feelings for a person,once that person has come of age,or vice versa,but that doesn't mean that they wanted them since childhood,tho some might and do,i'll admit that.Truthfully,Mike is actually trying to fight his temptation for Jayden.Now i do think Jayden and Mike having something between them is kind of creepy in some ways,but in some ways i think it's kind of cute,and daring,no offense to anyone.

Now i must admit that the age differences between some couples can be creepy sometimes,but on a personal note,i had dealt with a guy twice my age before,older than me yea,but that same guy is still the only person on this planet at the moment that i had ever been in love with or shared one of my most passionate and intimate moments with,i didn't mean to divulge too much of my personal life,but i feel it was necessary.I also know a female person,no names would be mentioned out of privacy,but she once couldn't stomach this 10 year old boy she used to babysit down the street,she was 17 going on 18 at the time,once the boy turned 20 she happened to see him again on a street corner,now they have a 3 year old daughter,and are living together.This story is in no way glorifying pedophilia or justifying it,a 18 year old of consent and a baby,toddler,child are two different things,and this is in no way incest either,taboo yes.

Thank you for reading His uncles or His daddies? (sauna tale)

www.ingramcontent.com/pod-product-compliance
Lightning Source LLC
Chambersburg PA
CBHW030250290526
45785CB00001B/35